CASTLES

THE FINAL YEARS 1954-1965

Laurence Waters

Ian Allan
PUBLISHING

This book is dedicated to the memory of
Dr Geoffrey Smith,
railway photographer and friend.

First published 2015

ISBN 978 0 7110 3822 6

Published by Ian Allan Publishing Ltd, Hersham, Surrey, KT12 4RG.

Printed in China

Visit the Ian Allan Publishing website at *www.ianallanpublishing.com*

FRONT COVER **No 5034 *Corfe Castle* (81A) speeds past West Ealing on Friday 24 February 1962 with a down service to Worcester and Hereford. *Corfe Castle* was withdrawn from Old Oak Common on 21 September 1962.** *C. G. Stuart, Great Western Trust*

BACK COVER **The 10.05am stopping service from Bristol to Swindon departs from Mill Lane Halt, on Saturday 18 March 1961 hauled by ex-works No 5023 *Brecon Castle* (82C). (see page 100)** *Hugh Ballantyne*

Contents

Introduction 4

Acknowledgements 4

Western Region shed codes 5

Castles: The Final Years 6

1954 22

1955 29

1956 36

1957 43

Castles in Colour 1957-1965 49

Castles at West Ealing 66

1958 70

1959 80

1960 90

1961 99

1962 107

1963 114

1964 119

1965 and beyond 123

Introduction

In their heyday the 'Castles' were probably some of the most charismatic locomotives on Britain's railways. Whether by accident or design, the Great Western, and Collett in particular, got it right. The 'Castles' had that special look: their overall design seemed to be perfectly balanced, with their curved steam pipes and lined green livery, together with the extensive use of copper and brass, and the large curved nameplates certainly made them stand out from the crowd.

It is now 90 years since the first 'Castle' was built, and at the time of writing, some 50 years since the last one was withdrawn. During their 42 years of main-line operation the 'Castles' gained their reputation for good performance, fine running, and excellent economy. Even today the various preserved examples continue to attract attention from both the enthusiast and the general public alike.

The 'Castles' are probably my favourite class of locomotive, and to produce another book on the subject has been an enjoyable experience. The photographs I have selected were taken between 1954 and 1965, and I hope illustrate the 'Castle' class locomotives during a period when they were still being used on many of the Western Region's express services. The photos are placed in chronological date order; I have not attempted to include a picture of every member of the class, but instead I have tried to show 'Castles' working in a variety of locations over the Western Region.

Acknowledgements

I would like to thank the following individuals and associations for their help in compiling this book:

The late Hugh Ballantyne, Michael Berry, Jerry Coleman, Steve Cooper, Anthony Doyle, Frank Dumbleton, John D. Edwards, Peter Gray, Robin Isaac, Phillip Kelley, Mike Mensing, Mike Peart, Norman Preedy, the late Dr Geoff Smith, Peter Triggs, Derek Tuck, the Ian Allan Library and the Great Western Trust.

Locomotive repair details and allocations are taken from records held at the National Archive at Kew, and also from the Peto 'Castle' class locomotive records, which are now held by the Great Western Trust at Didcot Railway Centre.

Western Region shed codes

The codes given in the picture captions indicate where the locomotive was allocated on the date of the picture.

81A	Old Oak Common		84C	Banbury (2D 1963-66)
81C	Southall		84E	Tyseley (2A 1963-66)
81D	Reading		84G	Shrewsbury
81F	Oxford		84K	Chester
82A	Bristol Bath Road		85A	Worcester
82B	Bristol St Phillips Marsh		85B	Gloucester
82C	Swindon		85C	Hereford
83A	Newton Abbot		86C	Cardiff Canton
83B	Taunton			
83C	Exeter		87A	Neath
83D	Plymouth Laira		87E	Swansea Landore
83G	Penzance		87F	Llanelly (later Llanelli)
			87G	Carmarthen
84A	Wolverhampton Stafford Road			
84B	Oxley (2B 1963-67)		88B	Cardiff East Dock (88A 1963-65)

Castles: The Final Years

To trace the evolution of the 'Castles' we have to go back to around the turn of the last century. At that time Great Western passenger motive power comprised mainly 'Dean Singles' or 4-4-0 types such as the 'Atbara', 'Bulldog', 'City' and 'Badminton' classes. Capable as these locomotives were, with passenger numbers growing and the need for longer and heavier trains, they really did not have the pulling power needed, and double-heading often became the norm. This of course was both uneconomic and tied up valuable motive power.

G. J. Churchward took over from William Dean as Chief Mechanical Engineer of the Great Western Railway in 1901, and he soon set about designing new and more powerful locomotives that were capable of hauling these heavier trains. His aim was to introduce a range of standard two- and four-cylinder classes that would meet the needs of Great Western motive power for years to come. After much experimental work Churchward settled for a 4-6-0 six-coupled arrangement, deciding that with its greater adhesion and lower running costs this configuration would be more suitable for Great Western use. The first of his designs was the two-cylinder 'Saint' class 4-6-0, the prototype being introduced in 1902, with the remainder of the class appearing in batches between 1903 and 1913. With a tractive effort of 20,530lb, these were essentially mixed-traffic locomotives.

The first of the new four-cylinder locomotives, No 4001 *Dog Star*, rolled out of Swindon in February 1907. Including No 4000, the *North Star* prototype, which had initially been built as a 4-4-2 'Atlantic' for experimental purposes in June 1906, then converted to a 4-6-0 in 1909, some 61 'Stars' were constructed between 1907 and 1914. Fitted with Walschaerts valve gear, they were very successful and were supplemented by a further 12 locomotives built by Churchward's successor, C. B. Collett, during 1922/23. With a tractive effort of 25,090lb, the 'Stars' were much more powerful than the older 4-4-0s, while the new six-coupled arrangement also gave greater adhesion. Churchward had provided the Great Western with a series of fine two- and four-cylinder 4-6-0s, of which the 'Star' class represented the pinnacle of Great Western express passenger motive power at the time.

When C. B. Collett took over from Churchward as the Great Western's Chief Mechanical Engineer in January 1922, there was again a need for even more powerful locomotives. Probably because the 'Stars' and 'Saints' had proved so successful, there had been little in the way of new designs produced by the company for a number of years. Collett's answer to the problem of producing a more powerful locomotive was to use the basic 'Star' layout, and improve it by fitting a new larger but lighter (No 8) boiler. Collett's original idea had been to use the larger No 7 boiler, as in the '4700' class 2-8-0s, but this would have been too heavy. The new No 8 boiler had a firebox of the same size as the No 7 boiler but a smaller boiler diameter to reduce weight. The result became the 'Castle' class 4-6-0s, and when the first 'Castle' was built in 1923 its design had evolved from development work started by Churchward some 20 years earlier. The new class had many other up-to-date features, such as a better cab for the crew, and Collett also made use of many established standard parts. In many respects it could be said that the 'Castles' were just enlarged 'Stars'. The new engines, which were all fitted with outside steam pipes, produced a tractive effort of 31,625lb, substantially more powerful than the 'Star' class. The design was to provide the Great Western with a fine locomotive for its express passenger services, providing the 'Company' and latterly the Western Region of British Railways with some 40 years of excellent service.

It could be said that although Collett's 'King' class 4-6-0s became the flagships of the fleet, and hauled the heaviest loads, it was the 'Castles' that were the flyers and loved by enthusiasts everywhere. Interestingly, when the locomotives first appeared the Great Western publicity department proclaimed that they were 'Britain's Most Powerful Express Passenger Locomotive'. This only lasted until 1927 when this piece of publicity was switched from the 'Castle' to the new 'King' class locomotives.

Initially the 'Castles' were coupled to the standard design of 3,500-gallon tender, but from 1926 members of the class were supplied with a new and enlarged pattern 4,000-gallon tender. I personally think that the 4,000-gallon tenders gave the class a more balanced look.

The first 40 'Castles' built were initially allocated to Old Oak Common, Newton Abbot and Plymouth Laira, and were used on services between Paddington and the South West, but by the 1930s they were in use over many of the Great Western main lines. In 1935 the Great Western joined the craze of the time by fitting partial streamlining to 'King' class No 6014 *King Henry VII* and 'Castle' No 5005 *Manorbier Castle*, completely ruining the looks of

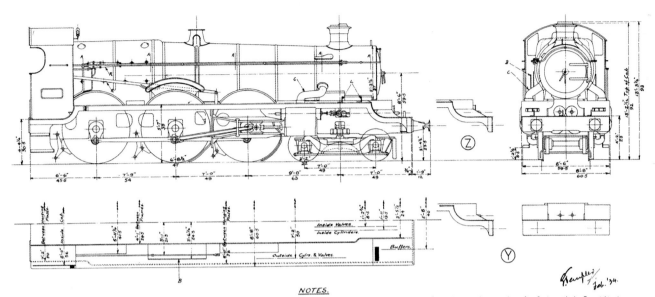

NOTES.

Diagram Y: Inside Valve Covers Nºs 4001-8, 4010-5 & 4017-20. Diagram Y: Inside Valve Covers Nºs 4021-30. Hand-rail knobs on left side given by centre lines A. Centre splasher B on right side set out to clear reverse rod: splashers on left side inline. External steam pipes C only fitted with new cylinders. Details marked L on left side only: those marked R on right side only. Wheel treads and flanges drawn to scale: allowances must be made for out-of-scale wheels. Dimensions in feet (full size) and in millimetres to the nearest half-m'metre for Gauge "0".

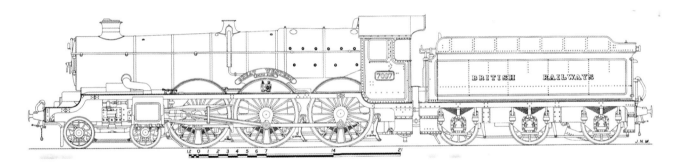

both locomotives. Thankfully common sense prevailed, and the horrendous exercise was soon abandoned.

On 25 April 1924 King George V accompanied by Queen Mary visited Swindon Works, and during the visit drove the then new No 4082 *Windsor Castle* from the works to the station. The Great Western saw the publicity value of this, and thereafter *Windsor Castle* became known on the Great Western as the 'Royal Engine', being used on many subsequent Royal duties. A small commemorative plate was affixed to each side of the cab after the Swindon visit. When the King died in 1936 No 4082 had the sad honour of hauling his funeral train from Paddington to Windsor.

On 6 February 1952 his successor King George VI died, and once again No 4082 *Windsor Castle* was requested to haul his funeral train. The locomotive, which was allocated to Worcester at the time,

TOP **The detailed drawing by Col Templer shows some of the many variations in the rebuilding of the 'Star' class.** *Reproduced from A Pictorial Record of Great Western Engines: Volume two – Churchward, Collett & Hawksworth Locomotives*

ABOVE **The last of the class to be completed at Swindon, No 7007 Great Western. Originally named** *Ogmore Castle*, **the name was changed in January 1948 with the coat of arms on the central splasher** *Reproduced from A Pictorial Record of Great Western Engines: Volume two – Churchward, Collett & Hawksworth Locomotives* was called to Swindon on 8 February, but was found to be in poor condition, having accumulated quite a high mileage since its last major overhaul in January 1951. This provided the Western Region with a slight problem, which was resolved by doing a swap. On 12 February Old Oak Common's No 7013 *Bristol Castle*, which was in much better condition, was called into the works, where it had its name and number plates removed and replaced by the name, number plates and commemorative cabside plates from *Windsor Castle*. In this guise it was used to haul the funeral train on 13 February 1952. The substitution did not go unnoticed, for after the funeral a number of letters appeared in the press spotting the switch. Apparently the Western Region was a bit embarrassed by this. It would have been an easy task after the funeral to swap the locomotives back again, but rather strangely this did not happen. However, the commemorative cabside plates were removed and not subsequently fitted to either locomotive. As a footnote, prior to the switch the real No 7013 was allocated to Old Oak Common, and No 4082 to Worcester. After the switch No 4082 (now 7013) went back to Worcester, and 7013 (now 4082) returned to Old Oak Common. No 7013 was eventually withdrawn on 6 February 1965, and there was some talk at the time of the Western Region changing it back to No 4082 *Windsor Castle* for possible preservation in the National Collection, but for whatever reason – perhaps because No 4073 *Caerphilly Castle* had already been preserved and also that No 7013 had been fitted with a double chimney – it never happened.

After nationalisation the 'Castles' continued to be the mainstay of motive power on many of the Western Region main-line services. The modernisation programme was still a long way off, and new motive power for Western Region services was provided by the construction of yet more 'Castles'. The success of the class saw F. W. Hawksworth, who had taken over the mantle of Chief Mechanical Engineer from Collett on 5 July 1941, continue their construction after the Second World War, with a further 40 'Castles' being constructed at Swindon in batches of ten: Nos 5098-99 and 7000-07 in 1946, then, after nationalisation, Nos 7008-17 in 1948, Nos 7018-27 in 1949, and the last batch, Nos 7028-37, in 1950. These 40 engines were known at Swindon as the '5098' class, as during their construction a number of improvements were made including the fitting of high-temperature Schmidt three-row superheated boilers in place of the old Swindon low-pressure types, and the provision of mechanical lubrication for the cylinders, valves and regulator. They were also fitted with a circular hole in the left-hand lower cab step, allowing rod access to the

hopper ashpan lever. Apart from these modifications they were essentially the same as the earlier members of the class.

Nos 7000-07 were fitted from new with an anti-carbonisation valve, situated on the right-hand running plate just ahead of the outside steam pipe. The modification was apparently not successful, and was not fitted to any other members of the class; it had been removed from all eight locomotives by about 1953.

No 7007 *Ogmore Castle* was completed at Swindon in July 1946 and was not only the last 'Castle' to be completed by the Great Western Railway, but also the last express passenger locomotive to be constructed by that company. After a suggestion by the late Ken Davies of the Railway Correspondence & Travel Society, No 7007 was renamed *Great Western* in memory of the old company. His suggestion was apt, as *Great Western* had also been the name of the very first locomotive to be entirely built at Swindon in April 1846.

From locomotive No 7008 *Swansea Castle*, which was completed in May 1948, the remaining members of the class were attached to the new Hawksworth-designed straight-sided 4,000-gallon tenders, which were similar in style to those fitted to the 'Modified Hall' and 'County' class 4-6-0s. Weighing in at 49 tons loaded, they were fitted from new to the last 30 'Castles'. Over the ensuing years many of these Hawksworth-designed tenders were also attached to a number of older members of the class.

'Castle' class construction came to an end in August 1950, 27 years to the month after the completion of No 4073 *Caerphilly Castle* (now preserved at the 'STEAM' Museum at Swindon). The last 'Castle' built was No 7037, being completed at Swindon on 28 August 1950. It ran nameless for a few months until it was officially named *Swindon* by HRH Princess Elizabeth on 15 November 1950, during an official visit to commemorate the golden jubilee of the borough. The coat of arms of the Borough of Swindon was also placed on the splashers under the nameplate.

The class eventually comprised 171 locomotives, of which 155 were new builds; of the remainder, No 111 *Viscount Churchill* was rebuilt from Churchward's 4-6-2 'Pacific' The Great Bear, and the others were conversions from older members of the 'Star' class. The rebuilding of the early 'Stars' was apparently quite a random process, undertaken as and when the locos needed new cylinders and boilers. It is interesting to note that apart from the break during the war years, 'Castles' had been in almost continuous production from August 1923 until August 1950, a record for any express passenger type, and a tribute to Collett's original design.

The first of the major changes to the 'Castle' class came in September 1947, when No 5049 *Earl of Plymouth* was fitted with a four-row improved superheater while in the works for an Intermediate repair; this provided a much higher superheat temperature of 660°F. In order to accommodate the bulky superheater header the chimney was moved forward. The subsequent improvement in water consumption, together with the potential of a longer boiler life, saw this modification gradually introduced to other members of the class. After the Second World War there was a decline in the quality of coal being supplied to the railways, and to compensate for this 'Castle' class smokeboxes were modified to improve the draughting arrangements. The alterations saw a reduction in the chimney liner and blastpipe diameters, and the removal of the Churchward-designed 'jumper top' on the blastpipe. A small 'improved draughting' plate was fitted in the cab of modified locomotives, and the initials 'ID' stencilled on the front running plate. After a number of fractures of the original-pattern outside steam pipe during 1954, a new curved design of the pipe was introduced, which generally alleviated this problem.

Further improvements to the class took place when on 15 August 1955 Landore-based No 7018 *Drysllwyn Castle*, built in May 1949, and an apparently indifferent performer, entered the test plant at Swindon for extensive testing. When it was released from the works on 15 May 1956 it had been fitted with an experimental double chimney constructed of sheet steel. At this time No 7018 was fitted with a three-row superheated boiler, but in July 1957 No 4090 *Dorchester Castle* was fitted with a four-row superheated boiler, a longer smokebox, a double blastpipe, and a new design of cast-iron double chimney. Again, as with the single chimney on No 5049, the new double chimney on No 4090 was moved forward to accommodate the superheater header.

On 24 January 1958 No 7018 again returned to Swindon where it was fitted with a four- row superheater boiler, the new design of double chimney, and a new improved mechanical lubricator that delivered some 50% more oil to the valves and cylinders. The smokeboxes of the modified locomotives were also equipped with self-cleaning apparatus, and a basket-type spark arrester. These modified 'Castles' could produce some 3,600lb of pull at 86mph on 20% cut-off.

This was effectively the final development of the 'Castle' class. When it left the works on 3 April 1958 No 7018 was transformed, becoming Bristol Bath Road's star performer, and being used extensively on the 'Bristolian' non-stop service to and from London.

The work at Swindon came to fruition when on 28 April 1958 *Drysllwyn Castle*, driven by Jimmy Russe of Bath Road shed with a seven-coach train, recorded the fastest 'Bristolian' run ever using steam traction, covering the 117.6 miles in just 93min 50sec. The 7.2 miles between Hullavington and Brinkworth were covered at an average speed of 98.2mph, with a top speed of 102mph near Somerford. Just four days later, on 2 May, Driver Russe and No 7018 equalled the record once again, this time with an eight-coach train.

As demonstrated by Nos 4090 and 7018, the fitting of these boilers, double chimneys and improved lubrication resulted in a substantial improvement in the performance of the class, particularly at a time of increasingly poor coal quality. Sixty-six members of the class were eventually fitted with double chimneys, the modification being undertaken on those locomotives that were at the time carrying four-row superheated boilers. Boilers were changed as and when a renewal was required, being done randomly throughout the class, which meant that No 4074 *Caldicot Castle*, built in December 1923, was fitted with a double chimney, and No 7037 *Swindon*, a BR Western Region example built in August 1950, was not. Interestingly, also converted were eight members of the class built between 1923 and 1926 – Nos 4074/80/87/88/90/93/97 and No 7013 (which of course was originally No 4082). With Government policy at the time set at removing steam traction, one wonders if the exercise was really worthwhile as some of the locomotives were withdrawn within months of modification. For example, No 5078 *Beaufort* was modified in December 1961, and withdrawn from Neath on 12 November 1962 having run just 34,714 miles since modification; another example was No 5027 *Farleigh Castle*, which was modified earlier in March 1961 but also withdrawn on 12 November 1962, completing just 65,000 miles in service. A number of others also completed less than two years in service before withdrawal. Apart from the performance improvements, it was said that another reason for the modifications was to extend the working life of those locomotives so fitted; if that was the case, their early withdrawal rather quashes the argument. There is no doubt that the balanced look of the single-chimney 'Castles' was completely altered with the fitting of double chimneys. This subsequent change in appearance has always divided opinion, but to the Western Region, having to run a railway with a gradual reduction in the supply of good-quality coal, the improvement in performance probably justified it.

Other modifications at this time saw five double-chimney members of the class – Nos 4087 *Cardigan Castle*, 4088 *Dartmouth Castle*, 5084 *Reading Abbey*, 7013 *Bristol Castle* (originally No 4082

Windsor Castle) and 7014 *Caerhays Castle* – being experimentally fitted with Davies & Metcalfe Patent valveless lubrication. The extra oil reservoir for this system was mounted above the lubricator on the right-hand side of the smokebox, the idea being to lengthen the periods between refilling, but for whatever reason the experiment was not extended throughout the rest of class.

'Castle' class names

From early Broad Gauge days, and right through to the end of the 19th century, the Great Western had a history of naming its passenger locomotives. During the 20th century the tradition continued, with Churchward's new four-cylinder 4-6-0 locomotives being named after stars; the first 11 names had been first used on many of the early broad-gauge locomotives. Although known as the 'Stars', other members of the class, which eventually numbered 73 locomotives, were named after knights, kings, queens, princes, princesses and abbeys.

The tradition was continued by Churchward's successor C. B. Collett, who named his new four-cylinder 4-6-0s after castles; accordingly the first ten built during 1923-24 were named after well-known such buildings on the system. The GWR obviously envisaged constructing a large number of locomotives, as prior to the 1925 batch being built a list, dated 9 January 1925 and probably compiled by the Publicity Department, was sent to the Chief Mechanical Engineer's department. This list contained the names of 138 castles, many of which, it must be said, were not on the Great Western system. Someone had obviously then checked the list, ticking off some 87 names that were identified as being on the Great Western. However of the 87 identified as being on the Great Western system only 59 were subsequently used, one of which was surprisingly 'Corfe Castle' which is not on the Great Western at all, being situated adjacent to the LSWR Swanage Branch in Dorset.

The Great Western, it seems, was always looking for good publicity, and suggestions for locomotive names from the public were not only considered, but probably encouraged. Letters from the public to the company make interesting reading. In one dated 23 February 1924, a Mr Colclough suggested the names *Aberystwyth Castle* and *Harlech Castle*, and both were subsequently used. In June 1924 a 15-year-old lad named R. Thornhill of Leamington Spa wrote to the Great Western suggesting five possible 'Castle' names: *Carnarvon Castle*, *Arundel Castle*, *Kenilworth Castle*, *Carisbrooke Castle*, and again *Harlech Castle*. Of these, Arundel, Carnarvon and Carisbrooke were not considered

by the company as they were not on the system, but the other two were used, *Harlech Castle* on No 4095, and *Kenilworth Castle* on No 4097. I bet the young lad was 'as pleased as punch'!

The Great Western usually published a list of the proposed names for new locomotives in the *Great Western Railway Magazine*.

Sometimes the locomotive naming policy was questioned, as in letter to the CME's department dated 30 August 1925 from a Rev W. A. Westall of Walthamstow, who asked, 'How many have heard of Nunney Castle?' The reply from the CME's department dated 1 September states, 'You would be surprised to know how many people are interested in the naming of engines, and of the trouble we take in making the selection in order to meet, as far as possible, the views of the public. That in answer to your question I may say that this is a very celebrated ruin well known in a large area, and was selected by special request.' In the same letter, the Rev Westall also suggested that the name *Oystermouth Castle* 'would be treated as a jest'. The reply from C. B. Collett suggests that the sender is 'not in touch with the people who live in that neighbourhood, although I may say I agree with you that many of the names, to me, seem unsuitable, in fact between ourselves, I had personally struck out Oystermouth but it has been adopted to meet the views of others concerned.' *Nunney Castle* was eventually used on No 5029, built in May 1934.

Records also show that changes were always being made as the various batches of 'Castles' were completed, with many of the names originally selected for particular locomotives in that batch being moved around or withdrawn, sometimes it seems for no apparent reason. For example, on the list dated 17 August 1926, giving the 'Castle' names allocated to Nos 5004 to 5012, no fewer than six were crossed out and changed. The same memo advises that the names allocated for No 5007 *Oystermouth Castle* and No 5012 *Wallingford Castle* should not be used at all. It has been suggested that *Oystermouth Castle* may have been carried on No 5007 for a short time, but I think this has now been dismissed as incorrect. Further memos also state that the names allocated for Nos 5027 *Exeter Castle*, 5032 *Wilton Castle*, 5053 *Hatherop Castle*, 5058 *Picton Castle* and 5067 *Wilton Castle* should also be dropped.

The first five 'Star'-to-'Castle' rebuilds – Nos 4000, 4009, 4016, 4032 and 4037 – all initially retained their 'Star' names, and the sixth, No 111 *Viscount Churchill* was rebuilt from Churchward's 'Pacific' *The Great Bear*.

However, subsequent changes saw former 'Star' No 4009 *Shooting Star* change both name and number to *A1 Lloyds* on 20

January 1936 (being altered again to No 100A1 *Lloyds* on 26 February 1936); No 4016 *Knight of the Golden Fleece* became *The Somerset Light Infantry (Prince Albert's)* in January 1938; and in March 1937 No 4037 *Queen Philippa* was renamed *The South Wales Borderers*.

Eventually, just like the 'Stars' the class received names other than castles, probably at the same time confusing members of the travelling public. In June 1937 it was decided to remove the 'Earl' names from the '3200' class 4-4-0s and place them on 'Castles' Nos 5043 to 5063. Yet another change took place during 1940 and 1941, when Nos 5071 to 5082, all originally named after castles, were renamed after Second World War aircraft. Interestingly, the original list of selected aircraft names, dated 31 August 1940, shows No 5077 as *Fairey*, and No 5081 as *Lockheed*; both names were subsequently altered to *Fairey Battle* and *Lockheed Hudson* respectively. The last batch of 'Star' rebuilds, from Nos 5083 to 5092, all retained their 'Abbey' names, but in May 1935 No 5086 *Malvern Abbey* was renamed *Sir Robert Horne*, being altered again in August 1936 to *Viscount Horne* (he was Chairman of the Great Western company from 1934 until 1940). The *Malvern Abbey* nameplates were not used again – apparently there was no abbey at Malvern, only a priory.

There were also a number that were named after various dignitaries and regiments, so in order to identify the class all of the non-castle names (except for the earls and regiments) had a small additional brass 'Castle Class' plate mounted on the splasher under each nameplate.

This renaming policy meant that by the late 1950s, apart from Nos 5064 *Bishop's Castle*, 5065 *Newport Castle*, 5067 *St Fagans Castle* and 5068 *Beverston Castle*, none of the other 42 locomotives, from No 5043 right through to No 5092, were named after castles – and of the 171 locomotives eventually built, only 115 carried 'Castle' names.

As and when other members of the class were renamed, the names generally cascaded down to newer locomotives. Nine names were used three times, and another 11 were used twice. Two names, *Denbigh Castle* and *Ogmore Castle*, hold the record, each being used on no fewer than four different locomotives. *Denbigh Castle* was carried by Nos 5049, 5074 and 7001 before finishing up on No 7032, while *Ogmore Castle* was originally allocated to No 5006 but was not carried; it was then used on Nos 5056, 5080 and 7007, before finally ending up on No 7035 (which had itself originally been allocated the name *Liddington Castle*).

ABOVE **This photograph shows the small plastic cabside plate that was fitted to some members of the class in the late 1950s when operating top-link duties. This example is seen attached to No 5054** *Earl of Ducie,* **and gives the driver's name and home shed, in this case 'Driver A. Perfect, Old Oak Common.' Mr Perfect was the driver of No 4079** *Pendennis Castle* **on the first leg of the 9 May high-speed special.** *Great Western Trust*

On 22 January 1948, in commemoration of the Great Western Railway, No 7007 *Ogmore Castle* was renamed *Great Western*, with transfers of the company coat of arms on each splasher. A month later, on 5 February 1948, No 7001 *Denbigh Castle* was renamed *Sir James Milne*, who had been the last General Manager of the company prior to nationalisation. Both locomotives were renamed without ceremony at Swindon Works. On 29 October 1948 No 7017 *Cranbrook Castle* was renamed *G. J. Churchward*, who was the CME of the Great Western from 1902 to 1921. It seems rather sad that although Churchward had a locomotive named after him, Collett and Hawksworth did not.

When No 5017 *St Donats Castle* was renamed *The Gloucestershire Regiment 28th 61st* in April 1954, the original name was not used again. The regimental name had been suggested by a Mr P. J. Edwards of the Gloucestershire Railway Society, and endorsed by Major C. R. Davis of the regiment. It was named at Gloucester station on Friday 23 April 1954, the anniversary of the Injin River Battle.

No 5066 *Wardour Castle* was officially renamed *Sir Felix Pole* at Paddington on Wednesday 4 April 1956, in remembrance of the Great Western's General Manager from 1921 to 1929, who had

ABOVE LEFT **No 5017** *The Gloucestershire Regiment 28th 61st*

ABOVE RIGHT **No 4000** *North Star*

LEFT **No 4016** *The Somerset Light Infantry (Prince Albert's)*

passed away on 15 January 1956. The last 'Castle' to be renamed was No 7005 *Lamphey Castle*, which was given the name *Sir Edward Elgar* at Swindon on 15 August 1957, the 100th anniversary of the composer's birth.

Luckily for us all, most if not all of the 'Castle' class nameplates still survive in museums and private collections, both here and abroad.

Rundown and withdrawals

Interestingly, in April 1950, some months before the last 'Castle', No 7037 *Swindon*, was completed, the first member of the class, No 100A1 *Lloyds* (originally No 4009 *Shooting Star*) was withdrawn. A further two, Nos 4016 *The Somerset Light Infantry (Prince Albert's)* (originally named *Knight of the Golden Fleece*) and 4032 *Queen Alexandra*, were withdrawn in September 1951, No 111 *Viscount Churchill* in July 1953, and No 4000 *North Star* in May 1957 – all except No 111 were rebuilds from earlier 'Star' class 4-6-0s.

The first 'proper' 'Castle' to be withdrawn was No 4091 *Dudley Castle* on 19 January 1959 from Old Oak Common. It had amassed

a mileage of 1,691,856 while in service, and had been one of the nine 'Castles' to be painted in the new BR experimental Apple Green livery in 1948. No 5086 *Viscount Horne* (originally named *Malvern Abbey*) had been withdrawn earlier, on 10 November 1958, but this was a 1939 'Star' rebuild.

A notable milestone came in September 1962 with the withdrawal of No 4037 *The South Wales Borderers*. This 'Star' class rebuild had the distinction of attaining the highest mileage of any Great Western locomotive, some 776,764 as a 'Star' and a further 1,652,958 as a 'Castle', a grand total of 2,429,722. No 4037 had been built in December 1910 and named *Queen Philippa*. It was rebuilt as a 'Castle' in June 1926, and renamed *The South Wales Borderers* in March 1937, probably at the request of the regiment. A quick calculation shows that it ran on average 46,725 miles for each of its 52 years of service. The highest mileage of any 'Castle' was probably achieved by No 4080 *Powderham Castle*, built in March 1924, which had completed a total of 1,974,461 miles prior to 31 December 1963, after which date mileage recording ceased. It was not withdrawn until 10 August 1964, by which time it may well have broken the two million mark.

The diesel-hydraulics were first introduced on West of England passenger services on 16 June 1958, when North British 'Warship' diesel-hydraulic No D601 *Ark Royal* hauled the down 'Cornish Riviera Express'; although a regular 'King' class working, 'Castles' were often used on this service. History relates that these early 'Warships' were not the most reliable of machines, probably resulting in the fact that during this early diesel-hydraulic period only 15 'Castles' were withdrawn, one in 1957, one in 1958, three in 1959, seven in 1960, and three in 1961. The introduction of the hydraulics meant that by 1961 almost all of the Class 1 passenger services between the South West and Paddington were hauled by these locomotives. In 1959 the Western Region's first diesel depot had opened at Newton Abbot, and this was followed in 1960 with another new depot at Plymouth Laira. The result was that by the spring of 1961 the allocation of 'Castles' in the Newton Abbot (83) division had dropped from 25 in 1959 to just 11 in 1961, and by August 1962 the few remaining 'Castles' in the South West were all working from Plymouth Laira, with eventually its sole survivor, No 7022 *Hereford Castle*, being allocated away to Hereford on 9 November 1963.

The introduction of the Summer 1959 timetable saw both the 'Bristolian' and 'Torbay Express' services, previously regular Class 1 'Castle' turns, succumb to diesel-hydraulic traction. 'Castle' No 5085 *Evesham Abbey* hauled the last steam-hauled up 'Bristolian' service to Paddington on 12 June 1959, with No 7024 *Powis Castle* working the last steam-hauled down train; from that date 'Torbay Express' services were diesel-hauled. However, the poor reliability of the hydraulic types saw 'Castles' substituting for them on many occasions, but by January 1961 all Paddington to Bristol services except the 9.45am up and the 4.15pm down, and including the weekdays-only 'Merchant Venturer' service to Weston-super-Mare, were in the hands of 'Warship' diesel-hydraulics. This resulted in a substantial reduction in the 'Castle' allocation at Bristol Bath Road. Interestingly, during October and November 1959 three of Bath Road's redundant 'Castles', Nos 4078 *Pembroke Castle*, 5057 *Earl Waldegrave* and 7011 *Banbury Castle*, were allocated to Banbury (84C) for use on Banbury-Paddington and Paddington-Wolverhampton semi-fast services. However, their stay at Banbury did not last long, and by April 1960 all three had departed to other depots. During September 1960 two other redundant Bath Road 'Castles', Nos 5073 and 5096, moved down the line to Taunton, where they were used on semi-fast services to both Bristol and the South West. The pair stayed at Taunton for just a year, moving away to Cardiff Canton during September 1961.

On 12 September 1961 Bristol Bath Road was closed to steam in preparation for the construction of a new diesel depot, and its few remaining 'Castles' were allocated to nearby Bristol St Phillip's Marsh. The new diesel depot was opened on 18 June 1962.

During the early 1960s 'Castles' were still providing the main motive power for many of the Paddington to South Wales, Cheltenham and Worcester services. However, another regular 'Castle' turn came to an end in September 1961 with the introduction of the new 'Blue Pullman' diesel sets on the previously steam-hauled 'South Wales Pullman' service. The last up train was hauled on 8 September by Neath-allocated 'Castle' No 4090 *Dorchester Castle*, with the down train leaving Paddington behind No 5048 *Earl of Devon*, also from Neath.

Cardiff Canton closed to steam on 7 September 1962, with its six remaining 'Castles' moving nearby to Cardiff East Dock. Yet another regular 'Castle' turn came to an end when on 3 November 1962 No 7034 *Ince Castle* hauled the 12.07pm service from Gloucester to Paddington. After this date the train was diesel-hauled..

The end of the Summer 1962 timetable saw an increasing number of main-line services dieselised. By this date the Western Region had taken delivery of some 160 'Warships', 'Hymeks' and 'Westerns'. This influx of diesel-hydraulic motive power resulted in the first of the big inroads into the 'Castle' class, with the en-bloc withdrawal during September 1962 of some 25 locomotives; during that year a total of 55 were condemned.

However, the 'Castles' could still show what they were capable of. Prior to the introduction of accelerated services over the Paddington, Birmingham and Wolverhampton 'cut-off' route (via Bicester), and in order to ascertain the condition of the track, on 15 May 1962 a high-speed test train was operated from Paddington to Wolverhampton and back. This was hauled by double-chimney 'Castle' No 7030 *Cranbrook Castle* from Old Oak Common depot. With a load of 108 tons, comprising just five coaches, which included the Western Region track recording coach, and with two firemen on the foot plate, No 7030 made the up and down runs in a total time of 224min 43sec, touching 96mph at Haddenham on the down run, and 103mph on the up run at both Bicester and Denham. This apparently is the highest speed ever officially recorded for the class. On the up run No 7030 covered the 60.8 miles from Leamington to High Wycombe in just 51min 59sec. Interestingly, prior to the run No 7030 had spent a short time out of use and in store at Old Oak Common. On 10 September 1962 steam traction was withdrawn from all fast services over the 'cut-off' route, and the majority of the Paddington to Birmingham via Bicester services were operated using the new 'Westerns' (later Class 52).

By the end of 1962 the only regular daily Class 1 passenger turns for 'Castle' class locomotives were on the Paddington to Oxford, Worcester and Hereford services.

The 'Cathedrals Express' was actually the last Western Region named train to be dieselised, remaining predominantly 'Castle'-hauled until the autumn of 1963.

A further 40 'Westerns' and 35 'Hymeks' (later Class 35) were delivered during 1963, and in the same year the first of the new Brush Type 4 (Class 47) diesel-electrics were delivered to the Western Region. By the end of 1964 more than 100 of these locomotives were being used on Western Region services and, together with the diesel-hydraulics, had taken over almost all of the remaining main-line 'Castle' workings, resulting in another major reduction in the fleet. Within just three years the class had been decimated with, as already mentioned, 55 being withdrawn during 1962, 48 in 1963, and another 37 in 1964. This left just 12 members of the class running on into 1965. Interestingly, with the high rate of 'Castle' withdrawals at this time (together with many other ex-Great Western 4-6-0s, of course) Swindon was unable to cope, and of the 171 'Castles' only 38 were actually cut up at the works. Three were preserved, but the rest were all sold to various scrap merchants throughout the country.

Another regular 'Castle' class turn came to an end when on Saturday 27 July 1963 Nos 5057 *Earl Waldegrave* and 7029 *Clun Castle* were used on the last steam-hauled Paddington to Newbury race specials. On the same date No 7036 *Taunton Castle* from Old Oak Common substituted for the regular diesel-hydraulic on a morning Paddington to Weston-super-Mare service.

Steam was withdrawn from the Paddington to Worcester services from Sunday 8 September 1963, mainly being replaced by 'Hymek' diesel-hydraulics. A day earlier, on 7 September, No 7023 *Penrice Castle* had the dubious honour of hauling the last official Class 1 'Castle' turn, the 11.10am up service from Worcester to Paddington.

On 1 January 1963 a number of regional boundary changes saw the Birmingham and Chester divisions transferred from the Western Region to the London Midland Region. This meant that 'Castles' allocated to Wolverhampton Stafford Road, and later at Oxley, were added to the London Midland Region book stock. At this date some 11 examples were still operating from Stafford Road, being used on some semi-fast services to and from Paddington, but mainly on the weekday and weekend cross-country services to and from Wolverhampton. The 11 comprised Nos 5022 *Wigmore Castle*, 5026 *Criccieth Castle*, 5031 *Totnes Castle*, 5063 *Earl Baldwin*, 5089 *Westminster Abbey*, 7001 *Sir James Milne*, 7012 *Barry Castle*, 7014 *Caerhays Castle*, 7019 *Fowey Castle*, 7024

Powis Castle and 7026 *Tenby Castle*. They were still ideal for this type of work, and the London Midland Region continued to operate them. Even after Stafford Road was closed on 9 September 1963 only three – Nos 5022, 5031 and 7001 were withdrawn – the remaining eight being transferred to nearby Oxley.

The demise of top-link work for the 'Castles' saw a number of the surviving locomotives moved around the system, often to sheds that did not previously have an allocation. In November 1963, and for the first time, four 'Castles' – Nos 5000 *Launceston Castle*, 5054 *Earl of Ducie*, 5055 *Earl of Eldon* and 7022 *Hereford Castle* – were allocated to Hereford, being mainly for use on the North-to-West services between Cardiff and Shrewsbury, and some Hereford-Worcester-Paddington services. Nos 5000, 5054 and 5055 had previously been placed into store, so were not perhaps in the best of condition on arrival at Hereford. The North West to Cardiff services were no easy task for a 'Castle', even in good condition, but after some attention at Hereford they generally performed well. After working from Hereford for a number of months, Nos 5054 and 7022 left for Worcester, being replaced at Hereford by Nos 5042 *Winchester Castle* and 5056 *Earl of Powis*, but by June 1964 Hereford's short-lived 'Castle' allocation came to an end, as one by one they departed to other depots.

On 20 June 1964, and in readiness for the summer weekend holiday traffic, the eight remaining 'Castles' at Oxley were joined by Nos 5000 *Launceston Castle* and 5054 *Earl of Ducie*, both previously at Hereford. At Oxley the 'Castles' continued to be used on weekend cross-country passenger services from Wolverhampton Low Level to the South via Oxford and Reading, as well as summer services from Wolverhampton to Bristol and the South West via Stratford-upon-Avon and Honeybourne. Another Oxley 'Castle' working was the Sundays-only Manchester to Plymouth service, the locomotive being used between Wolverhampton and Bristol. The 'Castles' also saw use on freight and parcels traffic around the West Midlands. It must be said that at this time many of the surviving members of the class were in poor external condition, and many had lost their name and number plates.

In March 1964, and with the 'Castle' class rapidly diminishing in numbers, the Western Region decided to run a special train to commemorate the 60th anniversary of *City of Truro*'s high-speed run. In the weeks preceding the event, members of the class were once again used on the Paddington to Worcester services, being rostered on the 9.15 down and the 1.15pm up. In order to assess their capabilities, locomotive inspectors had travelled on all of the 'Castles' still in operational condition that had run less than 40,000 miles since their last overhaul, eventually producing a shortlist of eight. These initially comprised Nos 5054 *Earl of Ducie*, 5057 *Earl Waldegrave*, 7008 *Swansea Castle*, 7022 *Hereford Castle*, 7023 *Penrice Castle*, 7025 *Sudeley Castle*, 7029 *Clun Castle* and 7032 *Denbigh Castle*, and of these Nos 5054 and 7025 still retained their single chimneys. All eight had been checked previously at either Worcester or Swindon MPDs to have their valves, pistons and valve gear removed and examined, and at the same time to have other faults rectified; this work was undertaken at depots due to the fact that by 1964 Swindon was not undertaking either Intermediate or General repairs.

No 5057 was removed from the list on 10 March 1964 when it was found to have cracked cylinder liners, being withdrawn on the same day. It was replaced by No 4079 *Pendennis Castle*; this was another single-chimney example, and had been originally omitted because of its age, although subsequent testing found it to be in excellent condition. The Worcester service proved to be a good test for the eight locomotives, and the inspectors' final order of preference was Nos 5054, 4079, 7029, 7023, 7008, 7032, 7022 and 7025. Accordingly, rostering for the 9 May special saw No 4079 placed on the Paddington to Plymouth leg, No 7029 on the Plymouth to Bristol leg, and No 5054 on the final leg from Bristol to Paddington. It says something for the class that two of the single-chimney examples, one built in 1924 (No 4079) and the other in 1936 (No 5054), should prove to be better than the other much newer double-chimney examples, No 7029 excepted. Interestingly, all three had Heavy General repairs at Swindon during 1962 – No 4079 in June, No 7029 in July and No 5054 in September. The selection of *Earl of Ducie* was a particularly interesting one, as during its short stay at Hereford it had proved to be an unreliable locomotive. Records show that it was out of action receiving unclassified repairs for 21 days between 18 December and 9 January 1963, and a further 54 days from 19 January to 23 March 1964. By the time of the railtour No 5054 had moved to Worcester, and here again it was initially out of action, receiving unclassified repairs for 15 days from 8 to 23 April 1964. Worcester had a long-standing reputation for turning out its 'Castles' in tip-top condition, and true to form the shed fitters worked their magic on *Earl of Ducie*, turning what seemed to be an 'ugly duckling into a very fine swan indeed'!

The railtour was a great success, although No 4079 shed its firebars near Lavington while travelling at 96mph, ending the day at Westbury shed and being subsequently withdrawn from service. The failure of the firebars was put down to the extra heat that was generated by the 'Ogilvie' coal being used on the day, but mainly because some of the bars were porous. The other legs saw excellent

running, with No 7029 travelling the 127.40 miles from Plymouth to Bristol in just 133.09 minutes, with a maximum speed of 92mph at Nailsea. The firemen on No 7029 commented after the run that, 'The engine was very free, and no effort was required to keep her steaming, and that the hardest job in fact was holding her back.' Single-chimney No 5054 certainly did not disappoint, covering the 117.65-mile Bristol to Paddington section in just 95.33 minutes, nearly 5 minutes under schedule. Reaching a maximum speed of 96mph at Little Somerford, the 29-year-old locomotive with more than 1.4 million miles under its belt maintained a speed of between 80 and 90mph all the way from Swindon to Old Oak Common, resurrecting once again memories of the old pre-war 'Castle'-hauled 'Cheltenham Flyer' and the later Western Region 'Bristolian' service. I am sure that the Worcester and Swindon men who had prepared these locomotives, No 5054 in particular, were very proud at what they had achieved.

The imminent demise of the class meant that 'Castles' were in great demand for railtours. *Earl of Ducie* proved to be a popular locomotive, probably because of its single chimney, as just one week later, on 16 May 1964, the Oxford University Railway Society ran its own 'Castle Farewell' railtour using No 5054. The tour covered some 325 miles from Paddington to Oxford, Worcester and Hereford, and on to Newport, returning via the Severn Tunnel and Reading. The loco, which was again in tip-top condition, hit 92mph at Honeybourne on the outward journey, and the same speed at Little Somerford on the return, maintaining speeds of between 75 and 81mph over the 25 miles between Twyford and Ealing Broadway. The Oxford University minute books show that *Earl of Ducie* cost just £40 to hire for the trip. Those were the days!

On 12 July No 5054 was used on yet another enthusiasts' special, running from Sheffield to Cardiff via Worcester and Hereford, and once again it performed very well. It had been built at Swindon in June 1936 as *Lamphey Castle*, being renamed *Earl of Ducie* in September 1937. Sadly, however, although Nos 4079 and 7029, both used for the 60th anniversary run, survived the cutter's torch, No 5054 *Earl of Ducie* did not, being withdrawn from Worcester on 24 October 1964 having amassed some 1,412,394 miles in service. Its Indian summer had ended, and it was cut up at Swindon during December of the same year, a sad end to an outstanding member of the class.

On 7 June 1964 No 7023 *Penrice Castle*, one of the initial eight selected for the high-speed run, but not used, broke new ground when it hauled a return Railway Correspondence & Travel Society railtour from Gloucester to the former Somerset & Dorset station at Bath Green Park..

In February 1965 the rapidly diminishing fleet was reduced even further when eight of the remaining 12 operational 'Castles' were withdrawn, leaving just four working survivors, Nos 5042 *Winchester Castle*, 7022 *Hereford Castle*, 7034 *Ince Castle* and 7029 *Clun Castle*. Of these, No 5042 was the last working single-chimney example, and all four were at that time working locally in the Gloucester area. Although devoid of number and name plates, No 5042 was instantly recognisable at this time as it sported a dented chimney, apparently received when it was damaged by a depot lifting crane. Completed at Swindon on 9 July 1935, its mileage up until 28 December 1963, after which date records ceased to be kept, stood at 1,399,221.

In June 1965 Nos 5042, 7022 and 7034 were also withdrawn, leaving No 7029 as the sole working example of the class. It became a regular performer on the 5.45am service from Gloucester to Cardiff, and also the 5.00pm service from Gloucester Central to Cheltenham St James. As the last remaining working 'Castle', it was obviously very popular, and was used on a number of steam specials. On 24 January 1965 it hauled a Stephenson Locomotive Society special from Birmingham to Bristol, and on 3 April it was again used on a Warwickshire Railway Society special from Birmingham to Swindon. One official duty took place on Friday 11 June 1965 when it hauled the last scheduled steam passenger service from Paddington over the 'cut-off' route, the 4.15pm stopping service to Banbury. It was used on yet another special on 5 September 1965 when it hauled a Worcester Locomotive Society railtour from Birmingham to Eastleigh and Weymouth. On 27 November it hauled the Western Region's last official 'Farewell to Steam' railtour from Paddington to Bristol and Gloucester Eastgate, being driven from Paddington by Driver Reg Williams of Old Oak Common depot. It was then used on the last steam-hauled service from Gloucester Central to Swindon. *Clun Castle*'s final official working in BR ownership was on 1 January 1966 when it hauled the 5.00pm service from Gloucester to Cheltenham; this was also the very last official 'Castle' class working. Interestingly, Western Region records show that it had been officially withdrawn a day earlier on 31 December 1965.

It was not quite the end, however, as on 4 March 1967, and now in private ownership, Nos 7029 and 4079 hauled steam specials from Didcot and Banbury through to Chester to mark the end of through working between Paddington and Birkenhead. No 4079 hauled the Ian Allan 'Birkenhead Flyer', taking the train from Didcot, with No 7029 hauling the 'Zulu' from Banbury.

Between August 1968, the official end of steam on the BR system, and October 1971 British Railways operated a steam ban, but this was lifted when between 2 and 9 October 1971 No 6000 *King George V* was used to haul a Bulmers special 'Cider Train' that ran on various days between Hereford and Tyseley via Didcot and Oxford, as well as from Birmingham to Olympia, and Olympia to Swindon. The success of the special resulted in the lifting of the main-line steam ban, and on 11 June 1972 No 7029 *Clun Castle* was used to haul a 'Return to Steam' special from Tyseley to Didcot and back – and, as they say, 'the rest is history'.

Preserved 'Castles'

Today eight of these fine locomotives have been preserved, some as static exhibits. One could say that had it not been for Messrs Mike Higson, Patrick Whitehouse and, later, Dai Woodham, only three examples of Churchward and Collett four-cylinder 4-6-0s would have survived.

The only Churchward four-cylinder 4-6-0 example to survive is 'Star' class No 4003 *Lode Star*. Built in February 1907, it was withdrawn from service by the Western Region in July 1951 and placed in store at Swindon Works, where it spent the next 11 years mostly in the Stock Shed until its transfer to the new railway museum at Swindon in 1962..

Two Collett-designed four-cylinder 4-6-0s were also designated for preservation by British Rail as part of the National Collection. One was 'King' class 4-6-0 No 6000 *King George V*, which was withdrawn in December 1962 and stored at Swindon Works until 1968, after which it went on loan to H. P. Bulmer, the Hereford cider-maker. After a number of years on display at the 'STEAM' Museum at Swindon it moved to the National Railway Museum at York, where it is on static display

The other Collett locomotive on the list was 'Castle' class 4-6-0 No 4073 *Caerphilly Castle*, the first of the 'proper' 'Castles' to be constructed. It was built in August 1923, and withdrawn from service at Cardiff Canton on 10 May 1960, having amassed some 1,910,730 miles in service. After withdrawal it was restored to GWR condition at Swindon Works, and fitted with a Churchward 3,500-gallon tender, No 1855. On 2 June 1961 it was presented to the Science Museum in London, becoming part of the National Collection. In 1996 it moved to Didcot where it was put on static display. Here it stayed until 1999 when it moved to Swindon for

RIGHT No 4073 *Caerphilly Castle* (86C) stands in the works yard at Caerphilly on Thursday 19 October 1959, having just been released from the works after a Light Classified repair. *E. Mountford, Great Western Trust*

subsequent display at the new 'STEAM' Museum, which opened to the public on 14 June 2000.

That would probably have been it, but another 'Castle', No 4079 *Pendennis Castle*, became the second of the class to be saved. Built at Swindon in February 1924, No 4079 had been selected to take part in the 1925 locomotive exchanges, working with great effect over LNER metals. After running for some 40 years on the both the GWR and BR Western Region, it was withdrawn on 9 May 1964, having failed at Westbury while working the first portion of the Western Region's high-speed special. Thereafter it was sold firstly to Mike Higson, and later to the Hon John Gretton and Sir William McAlpine. In April 1965 it visited Swindon Works, where it was repaired and repainted, after which it was kept for a time in the lifting shop at Didcot Railway Centre. Thereafter it moved around the country, running on a number of railtours and being kept at Market Overton and Carnforth. In 1977 No 4079 was sold once again, this time to the Hammersley Iron Co of Australia. Prior to departing for that country, it made its last run on a special from Birmingham to Didcot on 29 May 1977.

Once in Australia it operated excursion trains for a number of years, mainly over the 240-mile-long ironstone line in the Pilbara region of Western Australia. In 1994 it was placed in store, and in early 2000 it was offered by the Hammersley Iron Company to the Great Western Society at Didcot, with the provision that the society would ship it home. The money required was soon raised, and No 4079 returned to Great Western soil on 8 July 2000. It is currently undergoing an extensive overhaul at Didcot Railway Centre, and should be back in main-line condition in the not too distant future. Interestingly, when it went to Australia in 1977 the ship that transported it from the UK travelled east, and when it returned in 2000 the ship also travelled east, so *Pendennis Castle* has actually circumnavigated the world!

The third 'Castle' to be preserved was No 7029 *Clun Castle*. Built in May 1950, it was one of the last batch of ten to be built at Swindon. It was fitted with a double chimney in October 1959, and officially withdrawn from Gloucester on 31 December 1965. On 27 November of that year it had operated the Western Region's last official steam working from Paddington to Gloucester Eastgate,

ABOVE No 4079 *Pendennis Castle* stands in the works yard at Swindon after a Heavy Intermediate repair on Sunday 22 October 1961. *Great Western Trust*

and its last task was to haul the 5.00pm passenger service from Gloucester to Cheltenham. In January 1966 it was purchased in running order by Patrick Whitehouse, reportedly for a sum of just £2,400, its scrap value at the time, and moved to the Birmingham Railway Museum at Tyseley in March 1966. Interestingly, while in private ownership it saw occasional use on freight services between Bordesley and Banbury yards well into 1966. Since then it has operated on both national network and preserved lines, and is currently undergoing restoration at Tyseley Locomotive Works.

The mid-1960s saw hundreds of steam locos being withdrawn each month, with many being sold to private scrap companies. One such company was owned by Dai Woodham, who operated a scrapyard in the old Barry Railway sidings at Barry Docks. During 1963-64 he took delivery of five withdrawn 'Castles', Nos 5029 *Nunney Castle*, 5043 *Earl of Mount Edgcumbe*, 5051 *Earl Bathurst*, 5080 *Defiant* and 7027 *Thornbury Castle*. Over the ensuing years, one by one each of these once fine locomotives was purchased by various individuals and preservation groups.

No 5029 *Nunney Castle* was built at Swindon in May 1934 and amassed some 1,523,415 miles in service until withdrawn from Cardiff East Dock on 28 December 1963. It arrived at Barry in April 1964, and was subsequently rescued from Dai Woodham's scrapyard by the Great Western Society and others in 1976, being delivered by rail to Didcot. It was then restored to running order at Didcot Railway Centre, making its main-line debut in 1990. During this period the Society sold its share in the locomotive, and since then it has undergone two further major overhauls, and has also once again changed owners. The last overhaul was undertaken at Tyseley and was completed in April 2008. At the

ABOVE No 5029 *Nunney Castle* (81A) stands in the yard at Old Oak Common in May 1956. Recording number 608 indicates that it had probably worked up to London on the 6.25am service from Penzance. it is coupled to Hawksworth tender no 4086 *R. H. G. Simpson, Great Western Trust*

time of writing it has been successfully operating on main-line steam excursions, and also on a number of preserved railways.

Double-chimney example No 5043 *Earl of Mount Edgcumbe* was withdrawn from Cardiff East Dock on 16 December 1963, also arriving at Barry in April 1964. Built at Swindon in March 1936, and fitted with a double chimney in May 1958, it amassed 1,400,817 miles in service. It was rescued from the scrapyard in September 1973, initially for use as a source of spare parts for Tyseley's other double-chimney 'Castle', No 7029 *Clun Castle*. However, after a change of heart it was decided to try and restore the locomotive to running order. After a lot of fundraising, work to restore No 5043 was started in 1998, and after some 10 years of hard work it was steamed once again on 3 October 2008, 45 years after it had last turned a wheel under its own power. After a number of successful test runs, No 5043 was officially passed for main-line running on 26 October 2008, and since then has produced some wonderful main-line performances; in the author's view it has probably been the best-running of all the preserved 'Castles'. I am sure that one of the reasons for its popularity is that it has currently been restored to fully lined BR middle chrome green livery, and fitted with a smokebox number and shed plate – quite simply, an authentic livery for a 'Castle' with a double chimney, and exactly how many of us slightly older enthusiasts remember them.

No 5051 *Earl Bathurst* was built at Swindon in May 1936 and named *Drysllwyn Castle*; it was renamed in August 1937. After accumulating 1,316,659 miles in service, it was withdrawn from Llanelly on 26 May 1963 and, as already mentioned, also ended up in Dai Woodham's yard, in October 1963. Purchased privately by a Great Western Society member, it was delivered by rail to Didcot Railway Centre in February 1970. However, after the death of the owner it was sold to the Society, and after extensive restoration it returned to steam in 1980, successfully hauling many steam excursions over the system, and on many preserved lines. Since then it has undergone a second major overhaul at Didcot, once again being used on both the main line and many preserved railways. In 2008 its main-line boiler certificate expired, and it was put on static display at Didcot. At the time of writing there are no immediate plans to restore it to running order.

No 5080 *Defiant* was withdrawn from Llanelly in April 1963,

ABOVE No 5043 *Earl of Mount Edgcumbe* (81A) and an unknown 'County' class 4-6-0 depart from Chippenham with a down service to Bristol, circa 1959. *Norman Preedy*

and arrived at Barry in October of that year. Built at Swindon in May 1939, on withdrawal it had covered some 1,117,030 miles in service. It languished for 11 years at Barry before being purchased in 1974 by the Birmingham Railway Museum at Tyseley. It was initially moved to Gloucester for storage on 9 August 1974, and thereafter to Tyseley on 24 May 1975. In 1985 work started on the restoration, and in June 1988 the locomotive was returned to working order. With its single chimney, it was restored to Great Western livery, its number painted on the front bufferbeam, and in this guise it worked on both the main line and on many preserved railways. With the need for a major overhaul, it was put on static display, and is currently on loan to the Buckinghamshire Railway Museum at Quainton Road, where it can be seen inside the restored former LNWR Oxford Rewley Road station.

No 7027 *Thornbury Castle* was built at Swindon in August 1949 and withdrawn from Reading shed on 28 December 1963, after running some 728,843 miles in service. It arrived at Barry in May 1964 and was purchased from Dai Woodham by the Birmingham Railway Museum, leaving Barry for Tyseley in August 1972. In April 1989 it moved to the Dart Valley Railway at Buckfastleigh, and after a number of years in store was purchased by the Waterman Heritage Trust. It is currently kept at Crewe Heritage Centre, where it is a long-term restoration project.

LEFT No 5051 *Earl Bathurst* from Landore (87E) pulls away from Stratford-upon-Avon on Thursday 26 August 1954 with a through service from Swansea to Birmingham. *T. E. Williams, Great Western Trust*

TOP LEFT No 5080 *Defiant* **from Landore (87E) is pictured here awaiting its next turn of duty at Old Oak Common on Sunday 20 April 1958.** *Great Western Trust*

BOTTOM LEFT No 7027 *Thornbury Castle* **stands at Old Oak Common on Sunday 6 September 1953. It is coupled to Hawksworth tender No 4062.** *Great Western Trust*

ABOVE No 7029 *Clun Castle* **(83A) stands at Exeter St David's in 1961 with a down through service from the West Midlands to the South West.** *Great Western Trust*

1954

RIGHT **This splendid shot of ex-works No 7000 *Viscount Portal* (83A) shows it standing at Swindon in February 1954 with an up running-in turn to Didcot. It had just been released from the works after a Heavy Intermediate (HI) repair.**

G. F. Heiron, Great Western Trust

LEFT **No 5059 *Earl St Aldwyn* (83A) stands in the works yard at Newton Abbot on Saturday 20 March 1954, prior to travelling to Swindon Works for an HI repair. It is coupled to Hawksworth tender No 4007, and was withdrawn from Shrewsbury on 22 June 1962.**

Great Western Trust

RIGHT The down 'Pembroke Coast Express' passes West Ealing on Saturday 10 April 1954 hauled by No 7012 *Barry Castle* (87E). It is coupled to Collett 4,000-gallon tender No 2820. *Barry Castle* was withdrawn from Oxley on 11 November 1964. *C. R. Coles, Great Western Trust*

RIGHT Standing in the yard at Swindon Works on Sunday 27 June 1954, fresh from a Heavy Intermediate repair but minus smokebox number plate, is No 4078 *Pembroke Castle* from Swansea Landore (87E). No 4078 spent most of its later working life allocated to depots in South Wales and was withdrawn from Llanelly on 2 July 1962. *Great Western Trust*

LEFT No 5085 *Evesham Abbey* (82A) rounds the curve at Dr Day's Junction, Bristol, with the 12 noon service from Penzance to Manchester in June 1954. *Great Western Trust*

RIGHT No 5023 *Brecon Castle* is pictured here at Newton Abbot on Saturday 26 June 1954; it was allocated to Penzance (83G) at this time. *Great Western Trust*

BELOW A Paddington to Birmingham and Wolverhampton service is seen here near Fenny Compton on Sunday 11 July 1954 hauled by No 7033 *Hartlebury Castle* (81A). No 7033 was fitted with a double chimney in July 1959. *C. Oldham, Great Western Trust*

LEFT A pair of 'Castles' are seen at their journeys' end at Paddington on Monday 19 July 1954. On the left is the 'Pembroke Coast Express', the 1.00pm service from Pembroke Dock to Paddington, hauled by No 4078 *Pembroke Castle* (87E). On the right is No 5085 *Evesham Abbey* (82A) on 'The Merchant Venturer', the 4.35pm service from Weston-super-Mare to Paddington. *Norman Preedy*

RIGHT No 5015 *Kingswear Castle* stands on the turntable at Wolverhampton Stafford Road (84A), its home shed, on Tuesday 20 July 1954. No 5015 ended up at Cardiff East Dock, from where it was withdrawn on 5 April 1963. *Brian Morrison*

LEFT **Three 'Castles' await departure from Paddington on Saturday 31 July 1954. From left to right, they are No 7009** *Athelney Castle* **(87E) on the 10.55am 'Pembroke Coast Express' service, No 7031** *Cromwell's Castle* **(83D) on the 11.05am service from Paddington to Penzance, and No 5082** *Swordfish* **(81A) on the 11.00am Paddington to Penzance service.** *Great Western Trust*

LEFT **The 11.10am service from Milford Haven to Paddington enters Cardiff General on Saturday 14 August 1954 hauled by No 5082** *Swordfish* **from Old Oak Common (81A). Allocated to Old Oak Common since November 1952, it was withdrawn from there on 2 July 1962.** *Norman Preedy*

RIGHT **A group of young lads watch as No 5027** *Farleigh Castle* **passes Stapleton Road Junction, Bristol, on Thursday 26 August 1954 with the 4.33pm service from Bristol to Liverpool Lime Street. Allocated to Bristol Bath Road (82A) at this time, the locomotive was withdrawn from Llanelly on 12 November 1962. It was fitted with a double chimney in April 1961.** *Great Western Trust*

ABOVE No 5033 *Broughton Castle* from Chester (84K) stands on the turntable at Oxford in 1954. In this picture it is coupled to Hawksworth tender No 4082. No 5033 was a regular visitor to Oxford, working in on cross-country services from the North West. It was fitted with a double chimney in October 1960, and ended its days at Oxford, being withdrawn on 7 September 1962. *R. H. G. Simpson, Great Western Trust*

BELOW In this nice portrait of No 5079 *Lysander* from Newton Abbot (83A) as it stands at Exeter on Tuesday 31 August 1954 with the down 'Torbay Express', the 12 noon service from London Paddington, it carries the early BR-pattern headboard. *Great Western Trust*

LEFT No 5006 *Tregenna Castle* (81A) stands in the yard at Bristol Bath Road shed on Saturday 18 September 1954. The locomotive has been fitted with 'improved draughting', as can be determined by the small 'ID' stencilled on the lower front of the right-hand frame. *Tregenna Castle* was withdrawn from Carmarthen on 3 April 1962. *P. J. Kelley*

LEFT The 11.20am service from Penzance to Cardiff and Swansea skirts the seawall at Dawlish on Saturday 9 October 1954 hauled by 'Castle' No 7000 *Viscount Portal* and 'Hall' 4-6-0 No 5959 *Mawley Hall* (83G). Allocated to Newton Abbot at this time, No 7000 was withdrawn from Worcester on 28 December 1963. *Great Western Trust*

RIGHT A busy time at Badminton on Sunday 10 October 1954 as No 7021 *Haverfordwest Castle* from Swansea Landore (87E) speeds through on a service from Paddington to Carmarthen, passing 0-6-0 No 2224 (82C) standing in the up bay with a workmen's train.
Great Western Trust

1955

A fine shot of No 5006 *Tregenna Castle* **as it climbs past St Mary's Crossing Halt, near Chalford, after restarting from Brimscombe with the 11.45am Cheltenham to Paddington service on Saturday 9 April 1955. Allocated at this time to Old Oak Common (81A), the locomotive was withdrawn from Carmarthen on 3 April 1962.**
Great Western Trust

The 1.55pm service from Paddington to Pembroke Dock is seen here departing from Newport on Friday 15 April 1955 double-headed by 'Castle' No 5005 *Manorbier Castle* **(86C) and 'Britannia' 4-6-2 No 70028** *Royal Star* **(86C).**
Great Western Trust

ABOVE The 11.20am service from Bristol to Paddington arrives at the terminus on Saturday 7 May 1955, hauled by No 5025 *Chirk Castle* (82A). No 5025 ended its days at Hereford, from where it was withdrawn on 13 November 1963. *Norman Preedy*

BELOW This terrific shot shows an up parcels train from Gloucester to London, hauled by No 5042 *Winchester Castle* from Gloucester (85B), hard at work as it climbs the bank on the approach to Sapperton Tunnel on Monday 30 May 1955. *G. F. Heiron, Great Western Trust*

RIGHT **No 7017** *G. J. Churchward* **(81A) stands at Old Oak Common on Sunday 19 June 1955. It was originally allocated the name** *Cranbrook Castle*, **but was renamed on 29 October 1948. It was withdrawn from Old Oak Common on 4 January 1963.** *Great Western Trust*

ABOVE **The now preserved No 7027** *Thornbury Castle* **(81A) speeds past Iver (Bucks) on Saturday 25 June 1955 with the 13-coach 7.30am service from Truro to Paddington.** *P. J. Kelley*

LEFT **No 5079** *Lysander* **from Newton Abbot (83A) rounds the curve out of Teignmouth on Tuesday 2 August 1955 with a Plymouth to Paddington service.** *Norman Preedy*

LEFT Looking in excellent condition, No 5028 *Llantilio Castle* (83A) stands at Exeter St David's on Saturday 6 August 1955 with the 1.45pm service from Bristol to Penzance. It had visited Swindon for a Heavy General (HG) repair just a few months previously.
Norman Preedy

LEFT No 7033 *Hartlebury Castle* (81A) waits to depart from Exeter St David's on Saturday 6 August 1955 with the 7.15am service from Plymouth to Paddington. It is coupled to Collett 4,000-gallon tender No 2540. It was fitted with a double chimney in July 1959, and was withdrawn from Old Oak Common on 7 January 1963, having spent the whole of its 13-year working life at this shed.
Norman Preedy

LEFT An up stopping service from Swindon to Paddington waits at Reading on Tuesday 16 August 1955, hauled by No 5023 *Brecon Castle* from Plymouth Laira (83D). The locomotive had left Swindon Works a few days earlier after a Heavy Intermediate overhaul, and was being 'run in' on this service. *Great Western Trust*

ABOVE A large group of spotters watches as No 5078 *Beaufort* (83A) arrives at Bristol Temple Meads on Thursday 1 September 1955 with the 10.35am 'Cornishman' service from Penzance to Wolverhampton. It was fitted with a double chimney in December 1961.

Great Western Trust

BELOW A rather dirty-looking No 4081 *Warwick Castle* (87E) is pictured here between Over Junction and Oakle Street with a relief service from Newcastle to Cardiff on Saturday 10 September 1955.

Hugh Ballantyne

RIGHT It is journey's end for No 5040 *Stokesay Castle* on an unidentified service (left) and No 5045 *Earl of Dudley* on an up service from Wolverhampton, pictured at Paddington on Saturday 17 September 1955. *Norman Preedy*

BELOW RIGHT The 'Edward Curran Companies' works outing from Cardiff to London is seen here arriving at Paddington on Saturday 17 September 1955 hauled by No 5099 *Compton Castle* (86C). Edward Curran was a large South Wales engineering company, which at this time ran its annual works outings by train. No 5099 was withdrawn from Gloucester on 11 February 1963. *Great Western Trust*

ABOVE No 5037 *Monmouth Castle* (85A) arrives at Paddington on Saturday 17 September 1955 with the 11.30am service from Hereford and Worcester. One of Worcester's favourite 'Castles' at this time, it was eventually withdrawn from Bristol St Phillip's Marsh on 20 March 1964. *Norman Preedy*

BELOW A fine picture of the down 'South Wales Pullman' as it rounds the curve at Stoke Gifford on Monday 19 September 1955 hauled by No 7001 *Sir James Milne* (81A). Originally named *Denbigh Castle*, the locomotive was renamed in February 1948, and the *Denbigh Castle* nameplates were subsequently reused on new-build No 7032. No 7001 was fitted with a double chimney in September 1960, and withdrawn from Wolverhampton Stafford Road on 17 September 1963. *R. C. Riley, Great Western Trust*

1956

RIGHT **No 5003** *Lulworth Castle* **from Exeter (83C) stands in the works yard at Swindon on Sunday 22 January 1956 after a Heavy General repair.** *Norman Preedy*

BELOW **The 7.00am service from Paignton to Liverpool via Weston-super-Mare, hauled by No 5089** *Westminster Abbey* **from Plymouth Laira (83D), crosses the junction at Worle on Monday 26 March 1956; the closed station of that name can be seen in the centre background. No 5089 was withdrawn from Wolverhampton Oxley on 11 November 1964.** *Great Western Trust*

ABOVE No 5003 *Lulworth Castle* from Exeter (83C) approaches Teignmouth on Monday 2 April 1956 with the 11.15am stopping service from Newton Abbot to Exeter. No 5003 was withdrawn from Newton Abbot on 29 August 1962.
C. Hogg, Great Western Trust

LEFT An unidentified up fast service hauled by No 5059 *Earl St Aldwyn* from Newton Abbot (83A) stands at Taunton on Monday 16 April 1956, coupled to Hawksworth tender No 4001. No 5059 was withdrawn from Shrewsbury on 22 June 1962.
Great Western Trust

LEFT No 5021 *Whittington Castle* **83C) backs out of Paddington on Saturday 5 May 1956 en route to Old Oak Common, after working in with the 7.15am service from Paignton. Surplus to requirements at Plymouth Laira, it moved to Cardiff Canton on 22 September 1959, from where it was withdrawn on 2 September 1962.** *Great Western Trust*

BELOW An up Bristol service speeds through Southall in May 1956 hauled by the now preserved No 5029 *Nunney Castle* **(81A), which at this time was coupled to Hawksworth tender No 4086.** *Nunney Castle* **was withdrawn from Cardiff East Dock on 28 November 1963 (see the main text).** *Brian Morrison*

ABOVE No 7018 *Drysllwyn Castle* (82A) arrives at Paddington on Friday 15 June 1956 with the 11.45am service from Bristol. The locomotive is recently out of Swindon Works after being fitted with an experimental double chimney, fabricated from sheet steel with flat parallel sides and a copper cap. *R. C. Riley, Great Western Trust*

BELOW 'The Devonian', the 9.15am service from Paignton to Bradford Forster Square, is seen here at Newton Abbot on Tuesday 10 July 1956 hauled by No 5079 *Lysander* (83A). Not exactly a fast service, the down train departed from Bradford at 10.15am and arrived at Paignton at 7.15pm. Allocated at this time to Newton Abbot, No 5079 was withdrawn from Landore on 6 May 1960. *Norman Preedy*

TOP LEFT The 11.10am Milford Haven to Paddington service hauled by No 4082 *Windsor Castle* (81A) passes Court Sart Junction on Saturday 14 July 1956. *M. Hale, Great Western Trust*

BOTTOM LEFT No 5050 *Earl of St Germans*, allocated to Shrewsbury (84G), passes Tiverton Junction with the 9.10am service from Liverpool to Plymouth on Friday 3 August 1956. It was running at this time with Hawksworth tender No 4082. No 5050 was withdrawn from Bristol St Phillip's Marsh on 2 September 1963.
Great Western Trust

ABOVE A fine view of No 5028 *Llantilio Castle* from Plymouth Laira (83D) as it skirts the seawall at Dawlish on Thursday 9 August 1956 with the 14-coach 7.30am service from Penzance to Manchester. No 5028 was withdrawn from Plymouth Laira on 20 May 1960.

T. E. Williams, Great Western Trust

ABOVE No 7010 *Avondale Castle* (81A) arrives at Birmingham Snow Hill in August 1956 with the up 'Cambrian Coast Express', the 10.10 service from Aberystwyth to Paddington. No 7010 was fitted with a double chimney in October 1960. *Norman Preedy*

RIGHT No 5052 *Earl of Radnor*, from Cardiff Canton, prepares to depart from Swindon with the 1.50pm service from Paddington to Carmarthen in October 1956. No 5052 ended up at Bristol St Phillip's Marsh, from where it was withdrawn on 2 September 1962. *Norman Preedy*

1957

LEFT The down 'Royal Duchy' service, the 1.30pm from Paddington to Penzance, is seen here near Clink Road Junction, Frome, hauled by No 7031 *Cromwell's Castle* (83D) on Saturday 9 February 1957. No 7031 ended its days at Worcester, being withdrawn on 16 July 1963. *P. A. Fry, Great Western Trust*

BELOW A down parcels train from West London passes Farnham Road signal box, west of Slough, on Sunday 17 February 1957 hauled by No 4076 *Carmarthen Castle* from Chester (84K). In December 1957 the locomotive moved to Swansea Landore, and was withdrawn from Llanelly on 4 February 1963. *J. D. Edwards*

LEFT The 2.10pm service from Paddington to Wolverhampton hauled by No 5056 *Earl of Powis* (81A) is pictured here at Seer Green on the 'cut-off' route on Sunday 3 March 1957 – the station can just be seen behind the last coach. No 5056 was fitted with a double chimney in November 1960. *J. D. Edwards*

LEFT A pair of 'Castles' stand in the yard at Oxford in April 1957. On the left is No 5083 *Bath Abbey* (85A), and on the right No 5012 *Berry Pomeroy Castle* from Oxford (81F). The former was withdrawn from Worcester on 7 January 1959, and No 5012 from Oxford on 24 April 1962. *J. D. Edwards*

RIGHT The 6.45am service from Wolverhampton to Paddington is pictured here at High Wycombe on Thursday 11 April 1957 hauled by No 5010 *Restormel Castle* from Wolverhampton Stafford Road (84A). The locomotive was eventually withdrawn from Reading on 5 October 1959. *J. D. Edwards*

LEFT No 5061 *Earl of Birkenhead*, from Chester (84K), speeds past Harbury cement works sidings on Saturday 13 April 1957 with a down service from Paddington to Chester via Oxford. *J. D. Edwards*

BELOW The 4.45pm service from Cardiff to Paddington hauled by the now preserved No 4073 *Caerphilly Castle* (86C) passes Pengam Junction, Cardiff, on Sunday 2 June 1957. The train is being diverted from the up main to the up relief due to Sunday engineering work. No 4073 was withdrawn from Cardiff Canton on 10 May 1960 and restored as part of the National Collection.

R. O. Tuck, Great Western Trust

The main portion of the northbound 'Cornishman' service reaches the top of the climb from Stratford-upon-Avon to Wilmcote on the North Warwickshire line hauled by No 5047 *Earl of Dartmouth* on Saturday 15 June 1957 – this was a regular working for a Stafford Road (84A) 'Castle'. No 5047 was withdrawn at the end of the Summer timetable on 21 September 1962. *M. Mensing*

RIGHT The down 'Cambrian Coast Express' service, from Paddington to Aberystwyth and Pwllheli, climbs through Hatton behind No 7032 *Denbigh Castle* from Old Oak Common (81A) on Saturday 13 July 1957. No 7032 was fitted with a double chimney in September 1960, and was withdrawn from Old Oak Common, its one and only shed, on 7 September 1964. *Great Western Trust*

RIGHT No 5071 *Spitfire* from Newton Abbot (83A) approaches Taunton on Monday 15 July 1957 with the 3.30pm service from Paddington to Penzance. *E. Vincent, Great Western Trust*

LEFT The 6.20pm stopping service from Taunton to Exeter enters Tiverton Junction in the summer of 1957 hauled by No 7000 *Viscount Portal* from Newton Abbot (83A). The branch line to Hemyock can just be seen behind the train. *J. Davenport, Great Western Trust*

RIGHT Landore (87E)-based No 4094 *Dynevor Castle* speeds past Swindon Works on Sunday 18 August 1957 with the 3.55am boat train from Fishguard to Paddington. No 4094 was withdrawn from Carmarthen on 20 March 1962.
Great Western Trust

RIGHT An unidentified service, possibly to Bristol, prepares to depart from Paddington in 1957 hauled by No 5025 *Chirk Castle* from Bristol Bath Road. No 5025 ended its days in store at Oxford, from where it was withdrawn on 13 November 1963.
Norman Preedy

LEFT The 10.05am stopping service from Bristol to Swindon is seen here approaching Saltford on Saturday 23 November 1957 hauled by No 7015 *Carn Brea Castle* (82A). This service was regularly used as an ex-works running-in turn. Fitted with a double chimney in May 1959, No 7015 was withdrawn from Old Oak Common on 5 April 1963. *Hugh Ballantyne*

Castles in Colour 1957-1965

RIGHT 'The Cornishman', the 9.15am service from Wolverhampton Low Level to Penzance via Birmingham, Stratford-upon-Avon and Cheltenham, is pictured here leaving Wolverhampton Low Level on Friday 14 June 1957. The locomotive is No 4083 *Abbotsbury Castle* (82A), and the train comprises BR Mk 1 coaches in chocolate and cream livery. No 4083 was withdrawn from Bristol St Phillip's Marsh on 14 May 1964. *M. Hale, Great Western Trust*

LEFT Young admirers watch from the bridge at Three Beaches on the Kingswear branch as No 4096 *Highclere Castle* (83A) passes with the up 'Torbay Express', the 11.25am from Kingswear to Paddington, on Wednesday 3 September 1958. *M. Hale, Great Western Trust*

TOP LEFT No 5053 *Earl Cairns* (83A), with a Hawksworth straight-sided tender, crosses Broad Sands Viaduct with the up 'Torbay Express' in the summer of 1959. No 5053 was allocated to Cardiff Canton in 1961, from where it was withdrawn on 13 July 1962
Great Western Trust

BOTTOM LEFT The down 'Torbay Express' passes Brewham Siding signal box, between Witham and Bruton, on Friday 25 July 1959 hauled by No 5032 *Usk Castle* (81A). This locomotive was withdrawn from Old Oak Common on 7 September 1963.
M. Hale, Great Western Trust

ABOVE No 5079 *Lysander* (83A), complete with a full rake of BR Mk 1 coaches in chocolate and cream, is pictured near Torquay with the 'Torbay Express', circa summer 1959. Displaced from the South West by the new diesel-hydraulics, the locomotive was reallocated to Swansea Landore on 22 April 1960. *Great Western Trust*

TOP LEFT One of the 'Star' rebuilds, No 5090 *Neath Abbey* (81A), stands in the yard at Wolverhampton Stafford Road on Saturday 5 March 1960. The loco started life as 'Star' No 4070, with the same name, and was rebuilt as a 'Castle' at Swindon in April 1939. *M. Hale, Great Western Trust*

BOTTOM LEFT The 4.30pm service from Paddington to Truro, hauled by No 7006 *Lydford Castle* (81A), passes Castle Cary on Thursday 8 September 1960. *P. Fry, Great Western Trust*

ABOVE This nice portrait of No 4081 *Warwick Castle* from Llanelly (87F) was taken as it stood in the yard at Old Oak Common on Sunday 11 March 1962. *C. G. Stuart, Great Western Trust*

ABOVE No 7027 *Thornbury Castle* (85A) rounds the East Curve at Didcot on Tuesday 27 March 1962 with the up 'Cathedrals Express', the 7.45am service from Hereford to London Paddington via Worcester and Oxford. *Thornbury Castle* is now preserved, and is currently under long-term restoration at Crewe Heritage Crewe. *C. G. Stuart, Great Western Trust*

TOP RIGHT No 5064 *Bishops Castle* stands on the turntable at its home shed, Gloucester (85B), on Friday 13 April 1962. At this time it was running with Hawksworth straight-sided tender No 4006. In the background stands fellow Gloucester-allocated 'Castle'

No 7000 *Viscount Portal*. No 5064 was withdrawn from Gloucester on 21 September 1962, and No 7000 from Worcester on 28 December 1963. *C. G. Stuart, Great Western Trust*

BOTTOM RIGHT No 7021 *Haverfordwest Castle* (81A), coupled to Collett tender No 2846, stands in the yard at Old Oak Common on 26 April 1962. It had been fitted with a double chimney in November 1961. No 7021 spent almost the whole of its working life at Landore, and for a very short time Llanelly, before being allocated to Old Oak Common in January 1962; it was withdrawn on 9 September 1963. *C. G. Stuart, Great Western Trust*

ABOVE No 7022 *Hereford Castle* stands in the yard at Plymouth Laira, its home shed, on Sunday 29 April 1962. No 7022 ended up as the sole surviving 'Castle' at Laira, and was allocated to Hereford on 9 November 1963. One of the last members of the class, it was withdrawn from Gloucester on 25 June 1965.
C. G. Stuart, Great Western Trust

TOP RIGHT No 5038 *Morlais Castle* (81F), coupled to Hawksworth tender No 4083, climbs Hatton Bank on Saturday 7 July 1962 with a down cross-country service from Bournemouth to Wolverhampton Low Level. *M. Hale, Great Western Trust*

BOTTOM RIGHT This picture is not quite what it seems as No 7006 *Lydford Castle* (81A) passes Bathampton Junction with the 8.45am service from Paddington to Bristol on Saturday 14 July 1962. At this time the Monday to Friday 'Bristolian' service was diesel-hauled, but on Saturdays it remained steam-hauled, and the shed staff at Old Oak Common often placed the 'Bristolian' headboard on the **locomotive.** *P. Fry, Great Western Trust*

TOP LEFT Old Oak Common-allocated No 5001 *Llandovery Castle* stands alongside the ash road at Worcester on Monday 23 July 1962. Notice that the Hawksworth tender, No 4098, has been loaded up with ovoid coal. *C. G. Stuart, Great Western Trust*

BOTTOM LEFT No 4089 *Donnington Castle* (81A) waits to depart from Oxford on Friday 10 August 1962 with the 5.35pm service to Paddington. This was the fastest service of the day, with a 60-minute schedule for its non-stop run to Paddington. No 4089 ended its days at Southall, from where it was withdrawn on 7 September 1964. *C. G. Stuart, Great Western Trust*

ABOVE No 7003 *Elmley Castle* (85B) speeds past Iver (Bucks) on 25 August 1962 with the 'Cheltenham Spa Express', the 5.00pm service from Paddington to Cheltenham. No 7003 was withdrawn from Gloucester on 10 August 1964. *P. Fry, Great Western Trust*

ABOVE Wolverhampton Stafford Road-allocated No 7001 *Sir James Milne* (84A) stands at Wolverhampton Low Level on Friday 7 September 1962 with the last 'Cornishman' service from that station. From 10 September the service was routed away from the Western Region, running over the old Midland Railway route via Birmingham New Street and Gloucester. *M. Hale, Great Western Trust*

TOP RIGHT Still looking in good external condition is No 5033 *Broughton Castle* (81F), taking coal at Wolverhampton Stafford Road in preparation for its next turn of duty on Sunday 9 September 1962. It was withdrawn just five days later, on the 14th. *M. Hale, Great Western Trust*

BOTTOM RIGHT No 5071 *Spitfire* (82B) stands in the yard at Wolverhampton Stafford Road on Sunday 11 May 1963, after a Light Classified repair at nearby Stafford Road Works, hence the newly painted smokebox. *M. Hale, Great Western Trust*

LEFT No 7035 *Ogmore Castle* (81A) is pictured on the Frome loop line on Friday 31 May 1963 with the 4.15pm relief service from Paddington to Plymouth. *P. Fry, Great Western Trust*

BELOW The 8.30am service from Paddington to Penzance is seen at Blatchbridge Junction, Frome, hauled by Reading (81D)-based No 5018 *St Mawes Castle* on Saturday 1 June 1963. *P. Fry, Great Western Trust*

ABOVE The 3.15pm service from Paddington to Worcester, hauled by No 7023 *Penrice Castle* (85A), passes South Moreton Yard, Didcot, on Thursday 3 July 1963. The goods yard here opened on 2 May 1943, and closed in 1964. *Mark Yarwood, Great Western Trust*

BELOW Looking in poor external condition, No 5031 *Totnes Castle* from Oxley (2B) is seen on the Heath Town Junction line on Thursday 17 October 1963 with the stock for the 10.35am service to Paddington. The photographer has noted that No 5031 was being used on station pilot duty at Wolverhampton Low Level; it was withdrawn just five days later, on 22 October. *M. Hale, Great Western Trust*

ABOVE A fine portrait of No 5014 *Goodrich Castle* (81A) at its home shed, Old Oak Common, on 20 October 1963. At this time it was coupled to Hawksworth tender No 4046. On 14 June 1964 No 5014 was transferred to the London Midland Region, being withdrawn from Tyseley in February 1965. *C. G. Stuart, Great Western Trust*

BELOW No 7032 *Denbigh Castle*, coupled here to Collett tender No 2934, awaits its next turn of duty at its home shed, Old Oak Common, on 8 March 1964. This was one of the last 'Castles' to work from Old Oak, being withdrawn on 7 September 1964. *C. G. Stuart, Great Western Trust*

RIGHT No 5063 *Earl Baldwin* from Wolverhampton Oxley (2B) passes Honeybourne West Loop signal box on the Cheltenham to Stratford-upon-Avon line on Saturday 4 July 1964 with a through service from the West of England to Wolverhampton Low Level. *M. Hale, Great Western Trust*

BELOW The final scheduled steam-hauled passenger service from Paddington, the 4.15pm service to Banbury via Bicester, is seen here at North Acton on Friday 11 June 1965 hauled by the now preserved No 7029 *Clun Castle* (85B). *C. G. Stuart, Great Western Trust*

Castles at West Ealing

West Ealing was an excellent location for photographing main-line trains travelling at speed to and from Paddington, as well as locomotives on milk trains at the nearby milk dock sidings. The late Charles Gordon-Stuart took all the following photographs at this location.

ABOVE No 4076 *Carmarthen Castle* (87F) speeds through West Ealing on Wednesday 9 May 1962 with the 11.55am service from Paddington to Fishguard Harbour. *C. G. Stuart, Great Western Trust*

TOP RIGHT The heavily loaded 4.44am service from Fishguard Harbour to Paddington passes through West Ealing on Tuesday 18 December 1962 hauled by No 5092 *Tresco Abbey* (86C). No 5092 was rebuilt by the Great Western from 'Star' class No 4072 in March 1938. *C. G. Stuart, Great Western Trust*

BOTTOM RIGHT No 7007 *Great Western* (85A) makes a fine sight as it approaches West Ealing on Wednesday 9 May 1962 with the up 'Cathedrals Express', the 7.45am service from Hereford. Worcester shed staff had a reputation for keeping their 'Castle' allocation in tip-top condition. *C. G. Stuart, Great Western Trust*

ABOVE No 7009 *Athelney Castle* (85B), coupled to Collett 4,000-gallon tender No 2694, passes West Ealing with the 11.15am service to Cheltenham Spa on Friday 16 March 1962. It was withdrawn from Old Oak Common a year later on 23 March 1963. *C. G. Stuart, Great Western Trust*

BELOW Looking in top-class condition, and with its large nameplate, No 5017 *The Gloucestershire Regiment 28th 61st* (85B) stands at West Ealing milk dock on Saturday 24 February 1962. No 5017 was withdrawn just seven months later on 7 September 1962. *C. G. Stuart, Great Western Trust*

ABOVE No 7003 *Elmley Castle* (85B) was also photographed at the milk dock at West Ealing, on Wednesday 9 May 1962, waiting to depart with the down milk empties. This was often a Swindon ex-works running-in turn, and *Elmley Castle* had recently visited Swindon for a Light Intermediate repair. It survived for another two years, being withdrawn from Gloucester on 10 August 1964. *C. G. Stuart, Great Western Trust*

BELOW No 7023 *Penrice Castle* speeds through West Ealing on Saturday 24 February 1962 with the up 'Cathedrals Express' service to Paddington. No 7023 operated the last Class 1 'Castle' turn from Paddington on 7 September 1963 when it hauled the 11.10am down service to Worcester. *C. G. Stuart, Great Western Trust*

1958

ABOVE **A Westbury to Bristol local stopping service departs from Freshford station on Saturday 3 May 1958 hauled by No 4084** *Aberystwyth Castle* **(82A), coupled to Hawksworth 4,000-gallon tender No 4037.** *Aberystwyth Castle* **was withdrawn from Cardiff Canton on 11 October 1960.** *R. E. Toop, Great Western Trust*

RIGHT **No 5037** *Monmouth Castle* **(85A) stands outside A Shop at Swindon Works on Sunday 4 May 1958, having arrived for a Heavy General overhaul. No 5037 remained in service for another six years, being withdrawn from Bristol St Phillip's Marsh on 20 March 1964.** *C. G. Stuart, Great Western Trust*

ABOVE No 5028 *Llantilio Castle* (83D) prepares to leave Penzance in May 1958 with the 10.35am 'Cornishman' service to Wolverhampton Low Level. No 5028 was withdrawn from Plymouth Laira on 20 May 1960. *Norman Preedy*

BELOW The down 'Bristolian' service hauled by No 7018 *Drysllwyn Castle* (82A) speeds past Box station on Tuesday 6 May 1958. The engine is fitted with a double chimney, and is coupled to one of the two 3,800-gallon self-weighing tenders. Numbered 4127 and 4128, the tenders were built in February and March 1952 respectively, and were used on a number of different locomotives. No 7018 was withdrawn from Old Oak Common on 17 September 1963. *Great Western Trust*

LEFT A pair of 'Castles' are pictured at Taunton on Monday 12 May 1958. Standing in the platform is No 5024 *Carew Castle* from Newton Abbot (83A) with the 8.00am service from Plymouth to Crewe (with through coaches for Liverpool, Manchester and Glasgow). On the right is No 4098 *Kidwelly Castle*, also from 83A, with an up local stopping service to Bristol. No 5024 was withdrawn from Newton Abbot on 21 May 1962, and No 4098 from Old Oak Common on 28 December 1963. *Brian Morrison*

LEFT The now preserved No 7027 *Thornbury Castle* (81A) climbs towards Dainton Tunnel on Saturday 17 May 1958 with the up 'Royal Duchy', the 11.00am service from Penzance. *Thornbury Castle* was withdrawn from Reading on 28 September 1963, ending up in Dai Woodham's scrapyard. It is currently in store at Crewe Heritage Centre. *Hugh Ballantyne*

LEFT No 5038 *Morlais Castle* (84G) passes Little Mill Junction on the Hereford to Newport line just north of Pontypool Road on Monday 26 May 1958, with a through service from Liverpool to Plymouth. It moved to Oxford in May 1962, then to Reading in September, from where it was withdrawn on 17 September 1963. *M. Hale, Great Western Trust*

RIGHT The down 'Cathedrals Express', the 4.45pm service from London Paddington to Hereford, accelerates through Yarnton Junction in June 1958 hauled by Worcester (85A)-based No 4088 *Dartmouth Castle*. The Worcester-based 'Castles' were always turned out in pristine condition. No 4088 was fitted with a double chimney in May 1958, and withdrawn from Bristol St Phillip's Marsh on 14 May 1964. *J. D. Edwards*

RIGHT No 4083 *Abbotsbury Castle* (83A) departs from Newton Abbot on Tuesday 24 June 1958 with an unidentified down service to the South West. Displaced from the South West by diesel-hydraulics, No 4083 moved to Cardiff Canton (86C) in September 1961, being withdrawn on 19 December of that year. *J. Davenport, Great Western Trust*

RIGHT The up 'Pembroke Coast Express', the 1.10pm service from Pembroke Dock to Paddington, speeds past Alexandra Dock Junction, Newport, on 12 July 1958 hauled by No 7003 *Elmley Castle* (87E). On the right is '7200' class 2-8-0T No 7237 (86A) with an up freight. The locomotive was fitted with a double chimney in July 1961, and was withdrawn from Worcester on 10 March 1963. *M. Hale, Great Western Trust*

ABOVE No 5011 *Tintagel Castle* (83D) climbs Dainton bank on 13 July 1958 with a down service from Paddington to Plymouth. It was reallocated to Reading in March 1960 and to Old Oak Common in December, from where it was withdrawn on 4 September 1962. *Norman Preedy*

BELOW The 9.55am service from Fishguard to Paddington speeds through the Thames Valley near Maidenhead on Saturday 2 August 1958 hauled by No 4082 *Windsor Castle* (81A). As described in the main text, this locomotive swapped identities with No 7013 *Bristol Castle* in February 1952, and was withdrawn from Old Oak Common on 2 July 1962. *Great Western Trust*

ABOVE The now preserved No 5043 *Earl of Mount Edgcumbe* (81A) approaches Bath Spa with the 8.45am 'Bristolian' service from Paddington to Bristol on Tuesday 19 August 1958. No 5043 had been fitted with a double chimney in May 1958. *Hugh Ballantyne*

BELOW Also photographed on 19 August, No 5090 *Neath Abbey* (82A) approaches Bathampton with the 10.30am through service from Cardiff to Portsmouth. This service was a regular turn for a Bath Road 'Hall' or 'Castle'. *Neath Abbey* was withdrawn from Old Oak Common on 31 May 1962. *Hugh Ballantyne*

RIGHT No 7001 *Sir James Milne* (81A) is at the head of the down 'Torbay Express' on the West of England main line at Stoke Canon on 1 August 1958. *Norman Preedy*

RIGHT No 5070 *Sir Daniel Gooch* (84A) calls at Stratford-upon-Avon on 16 August 1958 with the 11.15am Saturdays-only service from Newquay to Wolverhampton. This was a regular turn for a Stafford Road 'Castle'. *Norman Preedy*

LEFT Waiting at Shrewsbury for its next turn of duty in August 1958 is No 5040 *Stokesay Castle* (81A). It will work the up 'Cambrian Coast Express' through to Paddington, probably taking over from a 'Manor' class 4-6-0. *Norman Preedy*

LEFT **The 8.00am service from Cheltenham to Paddington speeds though Ealing Broadway on Saturday 30 August 1958 hauled by No 4094 *Dynevor Castle* (87E).** *C. G. Stuart, Great Western Trust*

RIGHT **The down 'Torbay Express', the 12 noon service from Paddington to Kingswear, is seen here between Goodrington Sands Halt and Churston on Wednesday 3 September 1958, hauled by No 4096 *Highclere Castle* (81A). *Highclere Castle* was withdrawn from Old Oak Common on 7 June 1963** *Great Western Trust*

RIGHT **A good portrait of No 5051 *Earl Bathurst* (87E) as it stands at Old Oak Common on Sunday 21 September 1958. Originally named *Drysllwyn Castle*, it was renamed in August 1937. It was withdrawn from Llanelly on 24 May 1963, and moved to Dai Woodham's yard at Barry. The locomotive is now kept at Didcot Railway Centre (see the main text).** *R. C. Riley*

RIGHT A service from Birmingham to Birkenhead arrives at Wrexham General on Saturday 27 September 1958 behind No 5050 *Earl of St Germans* (84G), coupled to Hawksworth tender No 4093. No 5050 ended its days at Bristol St Phillip's March, from where it was withdrawn on 2 September 1963. *T. Lewis, Great Western Trust*

BELOW The up 'Torbay Express' hauled by No 7001 *Sir James Milne* (81A) prepares to depart from Kingswear on Thursday 2 October 1958. Standing at the quay is the F. Everard & Sons coastal vessel *Speciality*. *Great Western Trust*

1959

An unidentified up service from South Wales stands at Reading on Sunday 26 April 1959. The locomotive is No 4099 *Kilgerran Castle* **(87E), whose white-painted buffers were a feature of Landore 'Castles' at this time. No 4099 was withdrawn from Llanelly on 7 September 1962.** *M. Hale, Great Western Trust*

Pictured at Flax Bourton on Thursday 30 April 1959 is No 5053 *Earl Cairns* **(83A) with the 9.05am service from Liverpool to Plymouth. No 5053 moved from Plymouth Laira to Cardiff in September 1961 and was withdrawn from there on 13 July 1962.** *Great Western Trust*

ABOVE No 4080 *Powderham Castle* (83A), with double chimney, stands at Bristol Temple Meads with a stopping service on Wednesday 13 May 1959. Recently reallocated from Bath Road to Newton Abbot, it is seen here coupled to Hawksworth 4,000-gallon tender No 4083. *Great Western Trust*

BELOW A down service to Cardiff and Swansea speeds through Maidenhead on Sunday 17 May 1959, hauled by No 4097 *Kenilworth Castle* from Landore (87E). No 4097 was fitted with a double chimney in June 1958, and withdrawn from Landore on 6 May 1960. *M. Hale, Great Western Trust*

LEFT Looking in tip-top shape, No 7019 *Fowey Castle* (82A) speeds through Filton Junction, Bristol, with the up 'Bristolian', the 4.30pm service to Paddington, on Tuesday 19 May 1959. *Hugh Ballantyne*

CENTRE LEFT A Glasgow and Manchester to Penzance service arrives at Truro on Wednesday 20 May 1959 behind No 5078 *Beaufort*. Standing in the bay is 2-6-2T No 4547 (83E) on the 1.20pm service to Falmouth. No 5078 was allocated at this time to Bristol Bath Road (82A) and was withdrawn from Neath on 12 November 1962. *M. Mensing*

BOTTOM LEFT The 9.40am excursion from Paddington to Wolverhampton hauled by No 5044 *Earl of Dunraven* from Old Oak Common (81A) rounds the single line from Bearley station to Bearley North Junction on Sunday 24 May 1959. Trains to and from Wolverhampton were being diverted on this date, via Bearley and Henley-in-Arden, due to maintenance work on Rowington water troughs. No 5044 was withdrawn from Cardiff Canton on 3 April 1962. *T. E. Williams, Great Western Trust*

ABOVE No 5061 *Earl of Birkenhead* (81D) climbs the 1 in 150 incline out of Henley-in-Arden with the diverted 10.00am service from Paddington to Birmingham on Sunday 31 May 1959. It had been fitted with a double chimney in September 1958, and was withdrawn from Cardiff Canton on 21 September 1962. *Great Western Trust*

BELOW It is the end of an era as the last steam-hauled up 'Bristolian' service, hauled by No 5085 *Evesham Abbey* (82A), waits to depart from Bristol Temple Meads on Friday 12 June 1959. After this date the service was scheduled to be hauled by the newly introduced diesel-hydraulic locomotives. *Evesham Abbey* was withdrawn from Bristol St Phillip's Marsh on 14 March 1964. *Great Western Trust*

LEFT The last steam-hauled down 'Bristolian' service, headed by No 7024 *Powis Castle* (81A), is pictured here after arrival at Bristol Temple Meads, some 4 minutes early. The photographer had travelled on the train. *Hugh Ballantyne*

BELOW A 14-coach up Channel Islands boat train pulls away from Weymouth on Friday 12 June 1959 double-headed by No 7020 *Gloucester Castle* from Old Oak Common (81A) and '4300' class 2-6-0 No 5370 (84E). *S. Rickard, Great Western Trust*

ABOVE Although the 'Bristolian' service had been officially dieselised, many of the other fast services between Paddington and Bristol were still steam-hauled. Pictured here passing Box station on 20 June 1959 is No 5085 *Evesham Abbey* with the 1.15pm service from Paddington to Bristol. *P. Fry, Great Western Trust*

BELOW No 7006 *Lydford Castle* passes through Saltash station en route to Plymouth with the up Penzance to Paddington 'Cornish Riviera Express' in July 1959. Allocated to Plymouth Laira at this time, it moved to Cardiff Canton at the end of the Summer 1959 timetable, and was fitted with a double chimney in June 1960. It was withdrawn from Old Oak Common on 16 December 1963. *Great Western Trust*

LEFT No 7005 *Sir Edward Elgar* (85A) arrives at Ledbury on Saturday 11 July 1959 with the Hereford portion of the 1.45pm service from Paddington. The locomotive is apparently carrying the wrong running number! No 7005 was withdrawn from Southall on 7 September 1964. *Hugh Ballantyne*

BELOW LEFT Fresh from a Heavy General repair at Swindon Works, No 5071 *Spitfire* (85A) stands at Oxford on Saturday 18 July 1959 with the down 'Cathedrals Express', the 4.45pm service from Paddington to Hereford. No 5071 had been fitted with a double chimney in June 1959, and was withdrawn from Bristol St Phillip's Marsh on 22 October 1963. *R. W. Hinton*

RIGHT No 5018 *St Mawes Castle* from Reading (81D) departs from Oxford on Friday 15 August 1959 with an up semi-fast service to Paddington. The locomotive was withdrawn from Reading on 10 March 1964. The author can well remember seeing *St Mawes Castle* on station pilot duty at Reading on a number of occasions. *J. D. Edwards*

ABOVE In sparkling ex-works condition, No 7036 *Taunton Castle* (81A) hauls the down 3.35pm fish empties from Swindon to Hull and Grimsby, comprising one fish van and three guard's vans, pictured here at Kennington Junction near Oxford on Wednesday 12 August 1959. No 7036 had just left the works after a Heavy General overhaul, and the evening fish train was usually an ex-works running-in turn as far as Banbury. The locomotive had been fitted with its double chimney during that month, and was withdrawn from service at Old Oak Common, its only shed, on 9 September 1963. *Great Western Trust*

LEFT Looking in tip-top condition is No 5069 *Isambard Kingdom Brunel* (83D), seen here passing Sidney Gardens, Bath, on Tuesday 15 September 1959 with the Brunel Centenary train. Two extra coaches, both ex-GW Super Saloons, had been placed in the 1.15pm service from Paddington to take members of the Institute of Mechanical Engineers to Bristol for the celebration of Brunel's centenary. No 5069 had been fitted with its double chimney in November 1958, and was withdrawn from Plymouth Laira on 21 February 1962.
Hugh Ballantyne

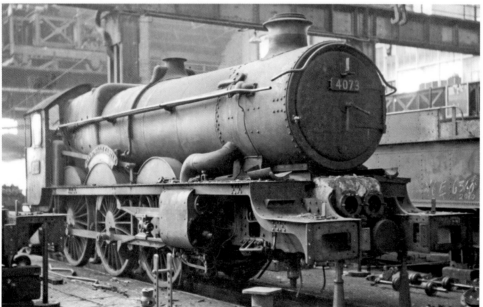

LEFT 'Castle' repairs were undertaken at Caerphilly Works from May 1958. Pictured inside the works erecting shop on Monday 28 September 1959 for a Light Casual repair is No 4073 *Caerphilly Castle* (86C), which was subsequently withdrawn from Cardiff Canton on 10 May 1960, and restored to its original as-built condition at Swindon, prior to becoming part of the National Collection.
Eric Mountford, Great Western Trust

RIGHT The 11.55am service from Paddington to Pembroke Dock speeds through Keinton Mandeville station on Monday 19 October 1959 hauled by No 7006 *Lydford Castle*. Allocated to Cardiff Canton (86C), it was withdrawn from Old Oak Common on 16 December 1963.
Great Western Trust

BELOW Apart from the up 'Bristolian' service, the fastest train of the day between Bristol and Paddington was the 11.45 up via Badminton. Pictured here with that service at Badminton on Sunday 22 November 1959 is No 4079 *Pendennis Castle* (82A); it was withdrawn from Bristol St Phillip's Marsh on 9 May 1964 (see the main text).
Hugh Ballantyne

1960

RIGHT **Pictured here on a frosty January morning in 1960 is No 7020 *Gloucester Castle* (81A) at speed near Chippenham with the 9.05am service from Paddington to Bristol. It was fitted with a double chimney in February 1961, and withdrawn from Southall on 7 September 1964.** *Norman Preedy*

ABOVE The 12.20pm service from Paddington to Bristol, hauled by No 7010 *Avondale Castle* (81A), is diverted into the up platform at Bath due to engineering works on the bridge on Sunday 28 February 1960; today this type of work would require both lines to be closed. No 7010 was fitted with a double chimney in October 1960, and was withdrawn from Reading on 10 July 1964. *Hugh Ballantyne*

ABOVE **Fresh from a Heavy Intermediate overhaul at Swindon, No 5040** *Stokesay Castle* **from Old Oak Common (81A) approaches Didcot on 5 April 1960 with the two-coach 11.55am local stopping service from Swindon, which was regularly used as an ex-works running-in turn. No 5040 was withdrawn from Bristol St Phillip's Marsh on 28 October 1963.** *W. Turner, Great Western Trust*

BELOW **The 6.20pm service from Chester to Shrewsbury arrives at Wrexham General on Easter Monday, 18 April 1960, hauled by one of Shrewsbury's (84G) 'Castles', No 5070** *Sir Daniel Gooch***, which was withdrawn from Old Oak Common on 20 March 1964.** *M. Mensing*

ABOVE **Speeding through Swindon in May 1960 is No 7035** *Ogmore Castle* **(85B) with the up 8.00am 'Cheltenham Spa Express' to Paddington. Including No 7035, the name** *Ogmore Castle* **was carried by four different members of the class.**
Norman Preedy

LEFT **The 12.55pm service from Paddington to Carmarthen and Fishguard runs through Didcot on Friday 20 May 1960 hauled by No 4099** *Kilgerran Castle* **(87E). Coupled to Hawksworth tender No 4046 at this time, it was withdrawn from Llanelly (87F) on 7 September 1962.**
Great Western Trust

ABOVE The tower of St Lawrence's parish church is seen on the skyline as No 7011 *Banbury Castle* (86C) passes through Ludlow on Wednesday 8 June 1960 with the 8.15am service from Bristol Temple Meads to Crewe. *C. P. Walker, Great Western Trust*

BELOW The down 'Pembroke Coast Express', the 10.55am service to Pembroke Dock, waits to depart from Paddington on Thursday 30 June 1960 hauled by No 4093 *Dunster Castle*. Allocated to Swansea Landore (87E), it is coupled to Hawksworth 4,000-gallon tender No 4056. *Dunster Castle* was one of the first of the class to be fitted with a double chimney, in December 1957. It was withdrawn from Gloucester on 7 September 1964. *Great Western Trust*

ABOVE No 7024 *Powis Castle*, from Old Oak Common (81A), passes Southall MPD in July 1960 with the down milk empties from West Ealing to the South West. *C. R. L. Coles, Great Western Trust*

LEFT The 6.25am service from Penzance to Paddington passes Brent station on 5 August 1960, hauled by No 4098 *Kidwelly Castle* coupled in front of a North British 'Warship' class Type 4. It is probably an understatement to say that these early 'Warships' were not the most reliable of locomotives. *Kidwelly Castle* was withdrawn from Old Oak Common on 28 December 1963. *Hugh Ballantyne*

ABOVE **Bristol Bath Road-allocated No 4077** *Chepstow Castle* **heads a down West of England service at Bristol Temple Meads on 12 August 1960. It was withdrawn from the city's St Phillip's Marsh depot on 13 August 1962.** *Norman Preedy*

RIGHT **The 11.55am service from Paddington to Milford Haven, hauled by No 4081** *Warwick Castle***, enters Llanelly on 30 August 1960. Records show that No 4081 was still allocated to Bristol Bath Road at this time, but was reallocated to Carmarthen on 19 September and withdrawn from there on 1 January 1963.** *A. Smith, Great Western Trust*

ABOVE No 4037 *The South Wales Borderers* (83A) arrives at Bristol Temple Meads with an up parcels service from the South West in August 1960. It has recently left Swindon Works after a Heavy Intermediate overhaul, and is coupled to Hawksworth tender No 4125. No 4037 had been rebuilt from 'Star' class No 4037 *Queen Philippa* in June 1926, and was officially renamed *The South Wales Borderers* at a special ceremony on 14 April 1937. It ran more miles in service than any other Great Western locomotive: 776,764 miles as a 'Star' and 1,652,958 miles as a 'Castle', a total of 2,429,722 miles. It was withdrawn from Newton Abbot on 17 September 1962. *Great Western Trust*

BELOW The 3.50pm milk train from Whitland to Kensington, headed by No 5067 *St Fagans Castle*, from Carmarthen shed, pulls out of Llanelly on 30 August 1960. It is coupled to Hawksworth straight-sided tender No 4032. *St Fagans Castle* was withdrawn from Reading on 13 July 1962. *A. F. Smith, Great Western Trust*

RIGHT The down 'Pembroke Coast Express' service from Paddington, hauled by No 5006 *Tregenna Castle* (87E), stands at Newport on 7 September 1960. *Great Western Trust*

BELOW Diverted because of engineering work on the 'cut-off' route, the 8.05am service from Birkenhead to Paddington runs through Oxford on Sunday 11 September 1960 hauled by No 5088 *Llanthony Abbey* (84A). It had been fitted with a double chimney in June 1958, and was withdrawn from Stafford Road on 21 September 1962. *M. Mensing*

RIGHT Another diversion on the same day, 11 September, finds No 5089 *Westminster Abbey* (84A) at Wheatley on the Oxford, Thame and Princes Risborough branch, with the 2.10pm service from Paddington to Birkenhead. The branch was used on many occasions as a diversionary route right up until its closure as a through route in 1967. *M. Mensing*

BELOW No 7016 *Chester Castle*, from Carmarthen shed, calls at St Annes Park station, Bristol, with the 9.50am down stopping service from Swindon to Bristol on Friday 30 September 1960. The engine is on a running-in turn after a Heavy Intermediate repair at Swindon. *Norman Preedy*

1961

LEFT No 7037 *Swindon* (81A) makes a fine sight as it departs from Stroud in March 1961 with the 11.15am service from Paddington to Cheltenham Spa. The last 'Castle' to be built, it was withdrawn from Old Oak Common on 4 March 1963.
Great Western Trust

LEFT The up 'Capitals United Express' is seen here at Patchway on Friday 3 March 1961 hauled by Old Oak Common-allocated No 4078 *Pembroke Castle*. No 4078 moved to Llanelly on 13 June 1961, and was withdrawn from there on 2 July 1962.
Norman Preedy

ABOVE The 10.05am stopping service from Bristol to Swindon departs from Mill Lane Halt, east of Box, on Saturday 18 March 1961 hauled by ex-works No 5023 *Brecon Castle* (82C). It was withdrawn from Swindon on 11 February 1963.

Hugh Ballantyne

RIGHT No 5043 *Earl of Mount Edgcumbe* (81A), coupled to Hawksworth tender No 4007, stands on the turntable at Wolverhampton Stafford Road on Saturday 15 April 1961. It had been fitted with a double chimney in May 1958, and was withdrawn from Cardiff East Dock on 16 December 1963.

Great Western Trust

No 5052 *Earl of Radnor* **(82B), coupled to Hawksworth tender No 4055, stands over the ashpit at Bristol St Phillip's Marsh in April 1961. It was withdrawn from that depot on 21 September 1962.**
Great Western Trust

On Friday 2 June 1961 No 4073 *Caerphilly Castle* **was officially handed over to the Science Museum in London, becoming part of the National Collection. This picture of the official handover shows, from left to right, Dr Richard Beeching (Chairman of the BTC), Mr John Ryan (Member, Western Area Board), Dr P. Dunsheath (Ministry of Education), Mr D. Follett (Director of the Science Museum), and Mr R. F. Hanks (Chairman, Western Area Board).**
Great Western Trust

LEFT No 7014 *Caerhays Castle* (81A) runs from the Devizes branch at Holt Junction in 1961 with a diverted West of England service. No 7014 is fitted with an experimental Davies & Metcalfe patent valveless lubricator – the oil reservoir can be seen on the right-hand side of the smokebox. The locomotive had been fitted with a double chimney in February 1959, and was withdrawn from Oxley on 6 February 1965. *A. Tyson, Great Western Trust*

LEFT Worcester (85A)-based 'Castle' No 7011 *Banbury Castle* speeds through Cholsey & Moulsford station on Thursday 22 June 1961 at the head of the up 'Cathedrals Express' (A22), the 7.45am service from Hereford to London Paddington. It is seen here running with Collett 4,000-gallon tender No 2778. *Banbury Castle* was withdrawn from Oxley on 13 February 1965. *J. Davenport, Great Western Trust*

LEFT No 5084 *Reading Abbey* (81A) stands at Exeter St David's on Tuesday 27 June 1961 with a down fast service from Paddington to Plymouth. No 5084 was fitted with its double chimney in October 1958, and was withdrawn from Old Oak Common on 2 July 1962. *M. Hale, Great Western Trust*

ABOVE No 7004 *Eastnor Castle*, from Worcester (85A), speeds through Combe Halt on the 'Cotswold Line' with a down Worcester service in July 1961. Combe Halt opened on 8 July 1935, and is still in use today. *Rev R. T. Hughes, Great Western Trust*

BELOW The 9.50am stopping service from Swindon to Bristol arrives at Box Mill Lane Halt on Saturday 19 August 1961 hauled by No 4076 *Carmarthen Castle* from Llanelly (87F). The locomotive is ex-works on a running-in turn following a Heavy Intermediate repair. *M. Hale, Great Western Trust*

RIGHT Honeybourne Junction is pictured here in August 1961 as No 5001 *Llandovery Castle* from Old Oak Common (81A) and fresh from an HG overhaul at Swindon, speeds through with the down 'Cathedrals Express' service. No 5001 was fitted with a double chimney in July 1961 and was withdrawn from Old Oak Common on 2 January 1963. *Great Western Trust*

RIGHT A Taunton to Plymouth stopping service calls at Exeter St Thomas station on 24 August 1961; the locomotive is Taunton (83B)-based No 5073 *Blenheim*. Records show that No 5073, together with No 5096, were allocated to Taunton from 13 September 1960 until both moved to Cardiff Canton during September 1961. Originally named *Cranbrook Castle*, No 5073 was renamed in January 1941. It had been fitted with a double chimney in July 1959, and was withdrawn from Cardiff East Dock on 26 February 1964. *Great Western Trust*

RIGHT A fine shot of No 7001 *Sir James Milne* (84A) leaving Ruabon on Friday 25 August 1961 with a service from Birkenhead to Paddington. Originally named *Denbigh Castle*, it was renamed in February 1948, and was withdrawn from Wolverhampton Stafford Road on 17 September 1963.
C. P. Walker, Great Western Trust

ABOVE The 9.00am service from Wolverhampton Low Level to Penzance, the 'Cornishman', is seen here near Warwick in September 1961 hauled by No 5072 *Hurricane* from Wolverhampton Stafford Road shed (84A); it was withdrawn from there on 30 October 1962. *Great Western Trust*

LEFT The last steam-hauled down 'South Wales Pullman' service from Paddington is seen here on Friday 8 September 1961 after arrival at Swansea High Street hauled by No 5048 *Earl of Devon* (87A). Standing in the adjacent platform is No 7016 *Chester Castle* (86C) on a parcels train. No 5048 was withdrawn from Llanelly on 14 August 1962, and No 7016 from Cardiff East Dock later that year on 26 November. *Hugh Ballantyne*

1962

LEFT The fitters take a break from working on No 5020 *Trematon Castle* from Cardiff Canton (86C) as it stands in the works yard at Caerphilly on Wednesday 14 March 1962. It had visited the works for a Heavy Casual repair and was at the same time fitted with new cylinders. It did not last for long, however, being withdrawn from Llanelly on 20 November 1962. *E. Mountford/Great Western Trust*

BELOW No 7010 *Avondale Castle* (81A) pulls into Newbury in around March 1962 with a down service to Taunton. *M. Peart, Great Western Trust*

RIGHT **Speeding past Southall MPD in April 1962 is No 5007 *Rougemont Castle* (85B) with a down service to Cheltenham. It was coupled at this time to Hawksworth tender No 4085. No 5007 was withdrawn from Gloucester on 4 September 1962.** *M. Peart, Great Western Trust*

LEFT **No 5096 *Bridgwater Castle* (86C), coupled to Hawksworth tender No 4061, stands in the yard at Cardiff Canton on Saturday 14 April 1962. Cardiff Canton was closed to steam on 7 September 1962, and No 5096 moved nearby to Cardiff East Dock. It was eventually withdrawn from Worcester on 15 June 1964.** *Great Western Trust*

LEFT **No 5043 *Earl of Mount Edgcumbe* (86C) and No 7026 *Tenby Castle* (84A) stand in the yard at Swindon on Monday 9 April 1962. No 5043 was in for a Heavy Intermediate repair, and No 7026 for a Light Intermediate.** *R. H. G. Simpson, Great Western Trust*

ABOVE 1962 was a bad year for 'Castle' withdrawals, with no fewer than 55 locomotives being taken out of service. Pictured here is the sad sight of six withdrawn class members outside A Shop at Swindon in May 1962. Of the 171 members of the class, just 38 were cut up at Swindon. As can be seen from the previous picture, while some were being repaired, others were being scrapped. *M. Peart, Great Western Trust*

BELOW At this time 'Castles' were still providing most of the motive power for the Paddington, Oxford, Worcester and Hereford services. Pictured here is No 7013 *Bristol Castle* (81A) emerging from Campden Tunnel on Saturday 19 May 1962 with the up 'Cathedrals Express' to Paddington. It had been fitted with a double chimney in May 1958, and was withdrawn from Gloucester on 6 February 1965. *Dr G. Smith*

LEFT No 5069 *Isambard Kingdom Brunel* stands in the scrapyard at Swindon where it was cut up during the week ending 19 May 1962. Fitted with a double chimney during December 1958, it had been withdrawn from service at Plymouth Laira on 21 February 1962.
M. Peart, Great Western Trust

BELOW The Hereford portion of the up 'Cathedrals Express' crosses the Worcester Viaduct and over the River Severn on its way into the city in the summer of 1962 hauled by Worcester (85A)-based No 7009 *Athelney Castle*. In the left distance is Henwick station. *Athelney Castle* was withdrawn from Old Oak Common on 22 March 1964.
A. Vickers, Great Western Trust

RIGHT Standing in the yard at Worcester on 3 June 1962 is No 5008 *Raglan Castle* (81A), coupled to Hawksworth tender No 4115. No 5008 was withdrawn from Old Oak Common just a few months later on 7 September.
Great Western Trust

LEFT No 5061 *Earl of Birkenhead* (86C) approaches Salisbury in the summer of 1962 with a through summer Saturdays service from Cardiff to Portsmouth Harbour. The locomotive is attached to Hawksworth tender No 4114.
M. Peart, Great Western Trust

LEFT A Birkenhead to Paddington service via Chester restarts from Ruabon hauled by No 5095 *Barbury Castle* on Wednesday 11 July 1962. Allocated at this time to Shrewsbury (84G) it was withdrawn on 16 August 1962.
M. Pearson, Great Western Trust

ABOVE No 7006 *Lydford Castle* (81A) is at Bath Spa on Saturday 14 July 1962 with the 8.45am service from Paddington to Bristol. At this time the Mondays to Fridays 'Bristolian' service was diesel-hydraulic-powered, but on Saturdays during 1962 the train was still steam-hauled, and the shed staff at Old Oak Common often placed the 'Bristolian' headboard on the locomotive. *Hugh Ballantyne*

BELOW The same Saturdays 8.45am service from Paddington, hauled by No 5015 *Kingswear Castle* (81A) and carrying the 'Bristolian' headboard, is pictured after its arrival at Bristol Temple Meads on 21 July 1962. The locomotive was withdrawn from Cardiff East Dock in April 1963. *Great Western Trust*

RIGHT No 5023 *Brecon Castle* descends through the Stroud Valley at St Mary's Crossing Halt with a Paddington to Cheltenham service on Saturday 4 August 1962. In the foreground is the Thames & Severn Canal. *Brecon Castle* was withdrawn from Swindon on 11 January 1963. *Norman Preedy*

LEFT A down service to Plymouth hauled by No 5060 *Earl of Berkeley* passes Dawlish Warren on Saturday 22 September 1962. Allocated at this time to Old Oak Common (81A), No 5060 was withdrawn from there on 5 April 1963. It had been fitted with a double chimney in August 1961. *Great Western Trust*

LEFT The 12.07pm service from Gloucester to Paddington, headed by No 7034 *Ince Castle* (85B), departs from Gloucester on Saturday 3 November 1962. This was the last day of steam operation on this service. *Ince Castle* had been fitted with its double chimney in December 1959, and was withdrawn from Gloucester on 25 June 1965. *Norman Preedy*

1963

ABOVE Double-chimney No 5031 *Totnes Castle* from Wolverhampton Stafford Road (84A) approaches Knowle & Dorridge with a service from the South Coast to Birmingham and Wolverhampton on the same day as the previous photograph. No 5031 was withdrawn from Wolverhampton Oxley just five months later, on 15 October. *Great Western Trust*

BELOW No 4080 *Powderham Castle* (88A), coupled to Hawksworth tender No 4082, stands in the yard at Cardiff East Dock in May 1963. Fitted with a double chimney in August 1958, it was withdrawn from Southall on 10 August 1964. No 4080 ran more miles in service than any other 'Castle'; until records ceased on 31 December 1963 it had completed 1,974,461 miles, and may well have reached the 2 million mark by the time of its withdrawal. *Great Western Trust*

ABOVE No 5026 *Criccieth Castle* (84A) runs through Aynho (for Deddington) with the up 'Pines Express' from Wolverhampton Low Level to Bournemouth West on Monday 27 May 1963. The 'Pines Express' had been re-routed to run via Birmingham and Oxford from 9 September 1962. *Criccieth Castle* had been fitted with a double chimney in October 1959, and was withdrawn from Oxley in November 1964. *Dr G. Smith*

BELOW The 4.33pm service from Salisbury to Bristol arrives at Bath Spa on Friday 31 May 1963 behind the now preserved No 5029 *Nunney Castle* (86C). *Hugh Ballantyne*

LEFT An up freight from the Birmingham area runs through Oxford on Thursday 4 July 1963 behind No 5081 *Lockheed Hudson* from Cardiff East Dock (88B), coupled to Hawksworth 4,000-gallon tender No 4087. 'Castles' were increasingly being used on freight and parcels traffic at this time. No 5081 was withdrawn from Cardiff East Dock on 21 October 1963. *D. Tuck, Great Western Trust*

LEFT No 5057 *Earl Waldegrave* from Old Oak Common stands at Newbury Racecourse on Saturday 27 July 1963 after arriving with a race special from Paddington. This was the last day of steam operation on the Newbury race specials. Fitted with a double chimney in May 1958, No 5057 was withdrawn from Old Oak Common on 10 March 1964. *D. Tuck, Great Western Trust*

LEFT A Paddington to Bristol parcels train stands at Bath Spa on Monday 10 August 1963; the locomotive is No 5098 *Clifford Castle* (81A). At this time 'Castles' saw regular use on both parcels and freight services. No 5098 was fitted with a double chimney in January 1959, and was withdrawn from Reading on 15 June 1964. *Hugh Ballantyne*

LEFT The rather dilapidated shed building at Wolverhampton Stafford Road (84A) is pictured here on Saturday 24 August 1963. It closed to steam on 9 September, with most of its 'Castle' allocation moving to nearby Oxley. Seen here, from left to right, are Nos 7001 *Sir James Milne*, 5026 *Criccieth Castle* and 7006 *Lydford Castle*.
Hugh Ballantyne

LEFT A fine portrait of No 7008 *Swansea Castle* in the yard at Oxford (81F) on Wednesday 28 August 1963. *Swansea Castle* had been allocated from new to Oxford in May 1948, but moved away to Old Oak Common on 25 February 1963. At Oxford it was used mainly on services to and from London, and also to Wolverhampton and Chester. It was withdrawn on 7 September 1964 having run just 483,663 miles up to the time that records ceased in December 1963, the lowest mileage of any 'Castle'.
D. Tuck, Great Western Trust

RIGHT Minus its smokebox number and shed plates, a rather grubby No 7004 *Eastnor Castle* (85A) approaches Oxford on Thursday 29 August 1963 with the 5.15pm service from Paddington to Worcester. No 7004 had been fitted with a double chimney in February 1958 and was withdrawn from Reading on 15 January 1964.
D. Tuck, Great Western Trust

BELOW The sad end of No 7021 *Haverfordwest Castle*, seen here stripped of any identification other than a chalked number and dumped at Oxford in April 1964. It had been fitted with a double chimney as late as November 1961, and was withdrawn from Old Oak Common on 9 September 1963; it remained in store at Oxford for a few weeks prior to being towed away to be scrapped at Cashmore's, Great Bridge.
Great Western Trust

LEFT Looking rather run-down, No 5098 *Clifford Castle* (81D) stands alongside the small lifting shop at Oxford on Saturday 18 April 1964; it was withdrawn just three months later on 15 June.
I. J. Hodson, Great Western Trust

RIGHT Withdrawn from service at Wolverhampton on Wednesday 17 June 1963, No 5022 *Wigmore Castle* awaits its fate in the yard at Cashmore's, Great Bridge, on 13 May 1964, having been sold to that company on 31 December 1963. Records show that some 36 'Castles' were cut up at Great Bridge. *M. Hale, Great Western Trust*

LEFT No 5054 *Earl of Ducie* (85A) leaves Hereford en route to Newport and the Severn Tunnel on Saturday 16 May 1964 with an Oxford University Railway Society special. No 5054 performed really well, hitting 92mph at both Honeybourne and Little Somerton. *D. Cape, Oxford University Railway Society, Great Western Trust*

LEFT No 7023 *Penrice Castle* from Worcester shed was also a popular choice for railtour use. It is seen here departing from Bath Green Park on Sunday 7 June 1964 with the return RCTS special to Gloucester. It had been fitted with a double chimney in May 1958, and was withdrawn from Worcester on 13 February 1965.
R. Nash, Great Western Trust

LEFT No 7019 *Fowey Castle* from Oxley (2B) is pictured here near Gloucester on 15 August 1964 with a Saturdays-only Wolverhampton to Plymouth service via Bristol. This was one of a number of 'Castles' allocated to Oxley at this time for working these services. One of the last few surviving members of the class, it was withdrawn from Oxley on 4 February 1965.
Norman Preedy

LEFT An up banana train, seen here near Biglis Junction, Barry, on Monday 17 August 1964, is hauled by No 7029 *Clun Castle*. At this time *Clun Castle* was coupled to Collett 4,000-gallon tender No 2621. The locomotive had been fitted with its double chimney in October 1959, and was withdrawn from Gloucester on 31 December 1965.
Great Western Trust

RIGHT Relegated to goods duties, No 5056 *Earl of Powis* is seen here at Hatton Junction with an up parcels service from the Birmingham area in August 1964. No 5056 had moved from Hereford to Oxley on 20 June, and was withdrawn from there just a five months later on 11 November. Notice the line of redundant guard's vans in the down sidings. *Great Western Trust*

RIGHT Minus its smokebox number plate, No 7024 *Powis Castle* from Oxley (2B) passes Aynho (for Deddington) on Saturday 8 August 1964 with the 10.42am service from Wolverhampton Low Level to Ramsgate. The high-level 'cut-off' route to Paddington can be seen in the background. This train was a regular turn for an Oxley 'Castle'. No 7024 was withdrawn from Oxley in February 1965. *P. J. Lynch*

BELOW RIGHT Still looking in good external condition after its exploits on the high-speed specials, No 5054 *Earl of Ducie* hauls a Saturdays-only through service to the South Coast via Oxford down Hatton Bank on 5 September 1964. Allocated to Worcester at this time, it was withdrawn from service just over a month later on 20 October. *Great Western Trust*

1965 and beyond

RIGHT No 5063 *Earl Baldwin* stands in the roundhouse at Newport Ebbw Junction (86A) on Thursday 14 January 1965, probably after working into Newport on a freight. The locomotive had been transferred to London Midland Region book stock on 30 December 1962, and was withdrawn from Wolverhampton Oxley in February 1965.

Great Western Trust

LEFT The last scheduled 'Castle'-hauled service from Paddington was the 4.15pm stopping service to Banbury via Bicester. Pictured here at Bicester North on Tuesday 13 April 1965 is No 7022 *Hereford Castle* (85B), devoid of all name and number plates and in appalling external condition, but operational. No 7022 had been fitted with its double chimney in January 1958, and was finally withdrawn from Gloucester on 25 June 1965.

Derek Tuck

ABOVE A sparkling No 4079 *Pendennis Castle* stands outside Swindon's A Shop in April 1965. It had been withdrawn on 9 May 1964 after failing at Westbury on the high-speed special. It had just been repaired and repainted in the works for its new owner, Mr Mike Higson. *Great Western Trust*

BELOW Another 'Castle' approaching the end of its working life is Gloucester (85B)-allocated No 5042 *Winchester Castle*, with its Hawksworth tender No 4101 full of coal and ready for its next turn of duty. It is pictured here at Banbury (2D) in May 1965, and was withdrawn from service just one month later on 25 June. *Mike Soden*

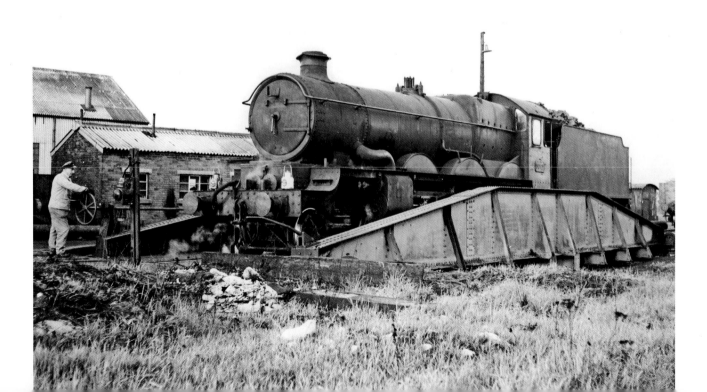

ABOVE No 7029 *Clun Castle* is pictured here at Gloucester on Saturday 26 June 1965 with the 5.45am service from Gloucester to Cardiff. This was a regular turn for *Clun Castle* at this time. *Great Western Trust*

LEFT Now privately owned, No 4079 *Pendennis Castle* prepares to depart from Paddington on Sunday 8 August 1965 with an Ian Allan railtour to Swindon Works. *P. Simpson, Great Western Trust*

ABOVE **The special ran via Gloucester and is seen here climbing Sapperton Bank on the same day.** *W. Potter, Great Western Trust*

RIGHT **Driver Reg Williams of Old Oak Common poses for photographers prior to taking No 7029 *Clun Castle* on the Western Region's 'Farewell to Steam' special from Paddington to Gloucester Eastgate on Saturday 27 November 1965.** *Great Western Trust*

LEFT Enthusiasts of all ages flock to see the 'Farewell to Steam' special after its arrival at Gloucester Eastgate.
Great Western Trust

BELOW No 7029 *Clun Castle* is seen again at Chester on Saturday 4 March 1967 after working one of the last-day 'Zulu' specials from Paddington to Birkenhead. No 7029 hauled the special onwards from Banbury. 'Zulu' was a title bestowed on the 4.45pm express service from Paddington to Birkenhead via Oxford, inaugurated in the 1880s.
R. Stevens, Great Western Trust

No 4079 *Pendennis Castle* worked a second special on that day and is seen here on the Ian Allan 'Birkenhead Flyer' at Rednal between Gobowen and Shrewsbury. Both Nos 4079 and 7029 were privately owned at this time. *V. Parry, Great Western Trust*